SOARING AS AN EAGLE
OVER LIFE'S CHALLENGES

SOARING AS AN EAGLE OVER LIFE'S CHALLENGES

DR. JOSEF A. HOWARD

authorHOUSE®

AuthorHouse™
1663 Liberty Drive
Bloomington, IN 47403
www.authorhouse.com
Phone: 1-800-839-8640

Published by AuthorHouse   06/18/2013

ISBN: 978-1-4817-6285-4 (sc)
ISBN: 978-1-4817-6284-7 (hc)
ISBN: 978-1-4817-6283-0 (e)

Library of Congress Control Number: 2013910573

CONTENTS

ENDORSEMENTS

It is my opinion that too many Christians do not understand the realness and seriousness of spiritual warfare and the tactics that the enemy of our soul uses against us to limit our thinking and stifle all that God has created us to be. My congratulations to Dr. Josef Howard for coupling scripture, nature's patterns, and such magnificent word pictures to help break down the wrong, limited, and destructive thinking we allow in our lives. This book will open any person's eyes to the potential and greatness that God desires for every human being through Jesus Christ. Every Christian inwardly desires to "*Soaring As an Eagle Over Life's Challenges*" and Dr. Howard brilliantly paints the picture of how that can happen through his book. This book is a must reading for any Christian!

Pastor Tim Burt
Associate Pastor, Living Word Christian Center

God, by His grace and because of His love for us, sometimes gives us second, third, and even a fourth chance in life. When given the chance to redeem our past, take hold of our present, and chart the course of events for our future, the decision to stay aground or to take flight and soar completely depends on us. By giving us another chance, God's desire is for us to brush off, make the necessary changes and take flight to the unlimited opportunities He has made available to us.

Dr. Howard has illustrated in this book God's plan for your life and a way out of your predicament. If you feel entrapped, frustrated, discouraged, tired, and defeated, this book is the key you need to begin to soar as an eagle through life's challenges. Read, spread your wings, and start living victoriously. Single women, this book is a must read to correcting all of your mistakes (past and present).

Trust me, if I knew what I know now as a result of reading this book, Oh lawd! How I would be gliding in life's hemisphere.

Munah G. Mombo, BBA

I have known Dr. Howard for about thirty-five years, since our paths crossed as little boys singing in a church choir in Liberia, West Africa. Over the past twenty-five years however, I have seen how God has cultivated Dr. Howard's life to be a great asset and blessing to the body of Christ around the world. In this book *Soaring as an Eagle*, Dr. Howard captures the anatomy of the eagle, turns it into ingredients that constitute the recipe of a sumptuous meal, and then spreads a table that is irresistible to the palate. "What may I give you for gratuity?" would not be a surprising question posed to Dr. Howard after you dine at this table, *Soaring as an Eagle*. Your perspective of life will definitely have a positive change when you walk through the corridors etched as they were, in the pages of this book.

Rev. Dr. Francis Tabla,
Pastor, Ebenezer Community Church,
Brooklyn Park, Minnesota, USA,
and Executive Director, Liberian Ministers
Association of Minnesota, USA.

Before the throne of the Most High, an eagle in flight occupy's a strategic position. In his new book, Dr. Howard unveils the life-transforming lessons revealed in the divine attributes found in this noble king of the birds. This is a must read for the church which finds herself wrapped up in the uncertainties of current global trends.

Apostle Edward E. Neepaye,
GO-GCAMI Global

Pastor Howard did it again! Here is another book that I know for sure will deeply impact lives in a lasting way.

When I first read the title, I thought I had already heard enough sermons on "soaring like an eagle." I was not prepared for how powerful, applicable and personal this book was going to be to me. Over and over, I found myself saying, "Amen!" and "Preach! Pastor, preach!" Each chapter is saturated with biblical wisdom, personal accounts and sage advice. However, far from "beating you over the head with the Bible," Pastor Howard gently and passionately implores the reader, as a loving father, to leave behind all "chicken" thinking and behavior, and instead whole-heartedly pursue a victorious "eagle" lifestyle.

Pastor Howard expresses the beauty and depth of a pastor's heart. His motivation is to empower God's people to set out on a straight, true course into the wise, abundant, victorious Christian life. He especially desires young people to make godly decisions at key, pivotal points in their lives. He wants to avoid meeting with them ten years later in his office, weeping, together sharing a box of tissues, and hear them say, "Oh, why did I do that? I wish somebody had warned me!"

This book is perfect for all high school, college, and young adults; those who are preparing to "take flight" in life. I hope every young adult has one parent, godparent, aunt, uncle or friend who loves them enough to impress this book upon them and urge them to read it. Truly, this book has the ability to change the course of someone's life, saving the reader from foolish decisions and much unnecessary grief.

God bless you, Pastor Howard, for this honest, practical, labor of love for the people of God!

Naomi Hard BA BSN RN FCN

FOREWORD

Dr. Howard's book, "*Soaring as an Eagle Over Life's Challenges*" is insightful, thought provoking, inspirational, motivating, and educational. In addition, it is well written and easy to read. Though this book focuses on the character, anatomy, domestic life, and other attributes of an eagle, it also compares and contrasts the life of an eagle to that of a man, ant, chicken, and snake. By so doing, Dr. Howard highlights some positive lessons on living above life's challenges, dealing with complicated relationships, strengthening one's leadership's ability, finding a life partner, raising a family, addressing complex issues in one's marriage, and growing as a Christian, just to name a few.

Many times, when we face challenges in life, we give up or give in so easily. I can attest to the fact that it is easy to walk away, succumb to the problem, or allow the devil to have his way without sometimes putting up a fight or waiting on God until we experience His divine intervention. Dr. Howard believes, as he shares in this book, that the challenges God allows us to experience are intended to mold us into who He wants us to become. These challenges are opportunities for growth and to prove that God is seated on the throne. He shares in this book that for every problem, there is a solution; for every mountain, there is a climber; for every attack, there is an attacker, and for any victory to be won, there must be someone willing to fight to the end. God has not called us to be weaklings. He calls us to be strong as Eagles, soaring the winds and not giving up at all.

Since I read this book, I cannot stop thinking about my relationships, habits and God-given abilities. God has so much in store for me and loves me dearly. He took His precious time to make me in His image and to enable me to live above and beyond the little challenges that I face in this life. Now I understand why the Psalmist says in Psalm 23:5: "He prepares a table before me in the presence of my enemies . . ." When my enemies are fighting to harm me, God is busy preparing a delicious meal for me because He knows that I have what it takes to overcome. That is the core message of this book!

Over the last few years, my family has faced what appeared to be insurmountable challenges in our health, educational pursuits, immigration, and even death in our family. There were times when I did not have the strength to go on and never thought I would live through another day. Many days I thought the Lord had abandoned my family. In our desperation, we called upon the Lord and He taught us through our father, Dr. Howard some of the principles and lessons that he has shared in this book. What you hold in your hand is a gold mine. It will transform your life as it did mine. I know that God is not done working on me yet, but I thank God that I am not where I used to be, thanks to the teaching I received about the life of an eagle. The same teaching is now yours. Read it, apply it, and you will see the difference.

Harris Sumo, BSW
Spiritual son to the Author

ACKNOWLEDGEMENTS

Words are inadequate to express my thanks and appreciation to my Lord and Savior Jesus Christ for saving me and giving me the wisdom, ability and farsightedness to pen what He placed in my heart. To Him I owe my life!

Special thanks to my colleagues in ministry, Pastor Tim Burt of Living Word Christian Center; Rev. Dr. Francis Tabla, Senior Pastor of Ebenezer Community Church; Apostle Edward Neepaye, General Overseer of GCAMI Global; Rev. Alexander Collins, Senior Pastor of Redeemed Life Church; and Rev. Becky Hanson, Chaplain at Regions Hospital, Saint Paul, Minnesota, who took their precious time to encourage me, read the original manuscript and provided valuable insights and corrections.

My deepest gratitude also goes to Munah G. Mombo who wrote one of the Endorsements for this book and Harris Sumo, my dear son, who wrote the Foreword. Thanks.

I must once again acknowledge the goodness of God towards me. He has given me a friend, neighbor, and a ministry companion in the person of Mrs. Naomi Hard. She worked with me from the very beginning of this book to the end. Sis. Naomi (as we affectionately call her) spent days reading, restructuring, correcting and praying over the original manuscript. What a friend! May God bless you for all you do, not only for my family, but also for the Kingdom of God.

I would like to express my thanks to my sweetheart and the love of my life, Lees, and our four loving children (Nancy, Cecil, Caleb and Marylyn). You have been my greatest and loudest cheering squad. Thanks for loving, believing, and supporting me. To all my spiritual children, I say, thanks as well.

My resolution for this year is that I will overcome poverty with productivity in both my ministry and personal finances by participating in a race where overtaking is allowed. Consequently, I joined one of the fastest growing multimillion-dollar companies in North America called 5Linx. It is enabling me to touch many lives and to also experience financial success. Special thanks to Vaughn and Candice Villafana, Lucie Matsouaka, Pastor Friday Onyeoziri and other leaders in the Eagle Team who have served as mentors for me since I joined this company.

To our spiritual parents in the Lord, Bishop Darlingston and Lady Chrys Johnson, Rev. Natt and Elder Margaret Friday, I say, thanks for being excellent examples for us to emulate.

Finally, I would like to express my thanks to you for acquiring this book. The fact that you are taking the time to read it is remarkable. There are many books out there that you could be reading, but you have chosen to read this one. May God bless you and open the eyes of your understanding as you read. I prophesy, in Jesus' name, that your life will never be the same after reading this book.

DEDICATION

This book is for those of you eaglets who have been intimidated and humiliated by the devil. You have succumbed to his lies to the point where you are afraid to leave your comfort zone, lack the courage to explore new avenues, soar through the sky, and glide with the wind.

I can guarantee that if you take the time and thoroughly read this book, it will change your life, break the chains of mediocrity, and cause you to realize that you are God's eaglet. Souring is in your DNA, ruling is your heritage, and the sky is your limit. Your life will never be the same!

INTRODUCTION

Six years ago, I preached a message entitled, "Soaring as an Eagle." I least expected that message to have ministered to people the way it did. I thought it would have been one of those sermons that people would have forgotten after a few minutes. It turned out to be one of few sermons to which people still refer to today around dinner tables, at family gatherings, and at church during Bible Studies. I have had numerous requests to preach it again, but I am very uncomfortable preaching the same message twice at the same church even if it is after several years. I have however preached the same sermon at three other churches and it has generated the same reaction. When some members of Bethel Word Outreach Church realized I was not going to preach the sermon again, they started to request that I write a book using the sermon's manuscript. I consented after several requests were made, and after spending time seeking the will of God. Hoping it would have been a "piece of cake" and believing that I had received a "green light" from the Lord, I embarked upon restructuring my sermon manuscript. As I did, I quickly realized that I had not done enough research and had not spent enough time in the presence of the Lord in order to produce the size and quality of book that I believed would be academically sound, theologically accurate, and spirit-filled, with moral imperatives and life-transforming principles. Consequently, what I thought would have taken me a few weeks or months lasted for a year and a half. After much prayer and research, I am convinced that the Spirit of the Lord has led me every step of this journey and has helped me in producing this book that is destined to transform lives in ways that are unimaginable.

"*Soaring as an Eagle Over Life's Challenges*" is a book that examines the life of an eagle and compares it to ours. Eagles are unique creatures with special abilities. They are recognized all around the world and many nations use them as their national symbol. They represent freedom, liberty, strength, power and majesty. On June 20, 1782, the bald eagle was chosen as the emblem of the United States most likely because of its long life, great strength and majestic looks. As expected, countless books have been written about eagles over the centuries and there are numerous references in the Bible regarding them, most notably, Isaiah 40:31 "But those who hope in the LORD will renew their strength. They will soar on wings like eagles; they will run and not grow weary, they will walk and not be faint."

Eagles are ordinary birds with extraordinary abilities. They possess characteristics that we ought to desire in our lives. For example, eagles are fearless, tenacious, and have excellent vision. Additionally, they fly high in the sky, enjoy life to its fullest while at the same time paying close attention to, providing for, and nurturing their young ones. As Christians, there are many things we can learn from eagles. This book explains how God would have us live our lives as Eagle Christians.

Chapter 1 analyzes the eagle's mentality in comparison to the chicken mentality. "Thank God I am not a chicken," could have also been a befitting title for this chapter. Have you ever thought of what life holds for a chicken? Do you know how chickens live their lives and how they think? This chapter will open your eyes to things you probably never thought about. After reading this chapter, you will be glad that the Lord compares you to an eagle and not a chicken. You will begin to change those mentalities associated with chickens and start thinking and behaving like an eagle.

Chapter 2 entitled, "Understanding the anatomy of an eagle," fully explains why God compares us to eagles and not to chickens. It highlights some of the skills, talents and abilities of eagles. However, the primary purpose of this chapter is for us to appreciate God for what He has given to us. When one examines the anatomy of an eagle and sees what it is capable of accomplishing because of its body structure, it becomes easy for that individual to look at himself and see the unlimited possibilities he has because of who the Lord has made him to be.

Chapter 3, "Understanding a few mysteries" is a chapter that critically examines Proverbs 30:18-19 which states, "There are three things that are too amazing for me, four that I do not understand: the way of an eagle in the sky, the way of a snake on a rock, the way of a ship on the high seas, and the way of a man with a young woman." This chapter examines these mysteries from both a spiritual and a natural perspective and highlights valuable lessons on how to "fly" as an eagle, be as wise as a serpent, navigate life's treacherous labyrinth, and love your family.

Chapter 4, entitled, "Understanding the Eagle's Perception of Marriage" is a must read for everyone. It is an "eye-opener" and a masterpiece. This chapters deals with how eagles find their mates (courtship), prepare to start a family, and take care of their young ones. It explains eagles' perception about marriage as a lifetime commitment. Those who desire to get married as well as those who are already married should read this chapter.

Chapter 5, entitled, "Understanding how eagles raise their family," deals with the intricacies and complexities of raising a family. It highlights the fact that both the male and female eagles play crucial roles in raising their eaglets. Moreover, it challenges us to rethink our roles as parents in the home and encourages us to become more involved in preparing our kids spiritually, educationally, emotionally, psychologically, and financially for the challenges that lie ahead.

Chapter 6, entitled, "Understanding how to rule as an eagle," examines man's role in the universe in general but also his specific God-given task as one who ought to rule and dominate over not only principalities and powers, but also rule over his household. The Psalmist declares in Psalm 8:4-7, "What is man that you are mindful of him, the son of man that you care for him? You made him a little lower than the heavenly beings and crowned him with glory and honor. You made him ruler over the works of your hands; you put everything under his feet." Chapter 6 answers this question in light of God's over-all plan for mankind. It explains the different learning stages and how to become an effective and efficient ruler. This is a chapter that every leader or anyone aspiring to leadership should read.

The concluding chapter is very practical, encouraging and uplifting. It examines how to react during a "valley experience." The truth is that every one of us has those "dark days" when everything seems to be against us. Eagles go through difficult times that experts referred to as the "molting stage." During that time, they feel depressed, abandoned, useless, powerless, and flightless. But, usually something happens and some of them rejuvenate. This chapter explains what occurs and how we too can get out of our "valleys of dry bones."

It is my prayer that this book will bless you, your family and those associated with you. Please do not just read it and place it on a shelf to collect dust. Share it with others and allow the Lord to minister to them through these words that I strongly believe were impressed on my heart by the Holy Spirit. May the Lord bless you and take you to your next level!

CHAPTER I

UNDERSTANDING THE EAGLE MENTALITY VS. THE CHICKEN MENTALITY

"But they that wait upon the Lord shall renew their strength;
they shall mount up with wings as eagles;
they shall run and not be weary;
and they shall walk and not faint" (Isaiah 40:31).

The Bible, God's inspired Word, is powerful, motivational, life transforming and at times mind-boggling. What I love most about the Bible is that it is always relevant to our situation and crosses the barrier of time. It has survived changes in cultures, norms, practices, ideologies, worldview and kingdoms. In it, one finds the answers to the most complex challenges in life. It is composed of prose, poetry, history, theology, personal letters and much more.

Through the Bible, God speaks directly to His people. In fact, the Bible is the primary way through which the Lord speaks to the heart of His children. The Bible is useful for teaching, rebuking, correcting and training in righteousness (II Timothy 3:16). When God speaks to us through His Word, He uses literary devices that make His thoughts easier to understand. Parables are one such device. Parables are short allegorical stories designed to illustrate or teach some truth, religious principle, or moral lesson.[1] Simply put, parables are heavenly truth with earthly significance.

In many cases in the Bible, the explanations of parables are given after the parables, for example, the parable of the sower (Matthew 13:3-23). At other times, the parables appear to be complex and offer little or no accompanying explanation. An excellent example is when the prophet Nathan tells David a parable of a rich man who steals a poor man's lamb (II Samuel 12:1-24). In the cases where we are not provided an explanation, we should pray for God to give us His "eyes" to see into the supernatural, ears to "hear" what the Lord is saying, and the mind to comprehend the spiritual implications.

---

[1]   Dictionary.com Unabridged
    Based on the Random House Dictionary, © Random House, Inc. 2011.

The apparent complexity of a parable should not discourage us from seeking its meaning and significance. It is a unique way of painting pictures with words. It is guaranteed that when we approach God with the willingness to listen, He will make known His will. The Bible declares in Psalms 25:9, "He guides the humble in what is right and teaches them His way." We are warned in Scripture that if we have "blinded" eyes, "heavy" ears and "dull" hearts, we will be unable to repent and be forgiven.[2] Praise God that He has not shut our ears, eyes and heart to His truth. Even when difficult parables are given without an explanation, God's Spirit is able to communicate to us the true meaning of the parable.

As we read the parables, we notice that God likens (associates or compares) His people with many things. In the Sermon on the Mount (Matthew 5), He compares believers to salt and light. He says, "You are the salt of the earth. But if the salt loses its saltiness, how can it be made salty again? It is no longer good for anything, except to be thrown and trampled by men. You are the light of the world. A city on a hill cannot be hidden."[3]

In John 15:1-17, we are compared to branches on a vine that the Father prunes in order for them to

---

[2]   Isaiah 6:9-10
[3]   Matthew 5:13-14

become fruitful. In Psalms 1, the Bible says that the godly are like trees planted by the streams of water which yields fruit in season and whose leaf does not wither. In John 10:11, Jesus said that He is the good shepherd and we are His sheep. Isaiah 53:6, says, "We all, like sheep, have gone astray, each of us has turned to our own way; and the Lord has laid on Him the iniquity of us all." In II Timothy, we are encouraged to be like good soldiers as we endure suffering.

It is therefore irrefutable that God uses parables to paint pictures in our minds about how He expects us to live and how to fully employ the skills, abilities and resources He has made available to us. Salt seasons food, light shines, branches produce fruit, sheep hear and follow their master, soldiers obey orders and endure hardship while seeking to accomplish at all cost their assigned mission. God has chosen to use the literary technique of simile (a figure of speech that indirectly compares two different things by employing the words "like", "as", or "than") comparing humans to items such as salt, light, branches and so forth. The challenge is that, in some instances, we are not fully aware of the function, ability, skill, and value of what we are likened to, and therefore we fail to grasp the message and meaning of what the Lord is trying to convey to us. Consequently, we read but do not understand and therefore cannot take hold of what

God has destined for us before the foundation of the world.

Before going further, allow me to illustrate the point that I want to make. In Proverb 6:6, the Bible says, "Go to the ant, you sluggard; consider its ways and be wise!" Later on in Proverb 30:25, the Word of God declares, "Ants are creatures of little strength, yet they store up their food in the summer." Do you see the implication? God wants us to learn from ants. Even though they are small, insignificant, nuisance, destructive, disliked and unappreciated, yet there are things God wants us to learn from them. Those who study ants (myrmecologists) have remarked that if we apply some of the simple principles ants apply daily; our lives would never be the same. Allow me to share four apparent principles with you.

The first principle learned from ants is that of **performance**. In order to perform with efficiency, there must be a plan and there must be full participation. When you watch a column of ants, you quickly realize that the ants seem to have a plan and there is full participation on the part of every ant. The ant colony is a community. Very seldom do you see an ant by itself. They work together to build colonies that are up to 35 feet below the ground. Because of their partnership, the ants are able to build a city in which there is a complex network of rooms, designated for various activities. This concept sharply contradicts our Western ideology of individualism. Ants, irrespective of size, shape or color, live together as a family and work cooperatively as a team to accomplish colony-wide goals. The question is, "Are we as 'colony–minded' as the ants, cooperating with others for common goals?" It is worth noting that a single ant is ineffective, weak, lazy and vulnerable; but a colony of ants is a force to be reckoned with.

The second principle learned from the ant is **partnership**. The ant colony is a community that works together for the greater good of all the ants. Indeed, there is sharing of food, facilities, and taking care of the younger ones. If you harass or try to kill an ant, the others will attack you, no matter what good reason you think you had (he was getting into your food or biting you). With no questions asked, their primary goal is to collaborate with the ant whose life is threatened to ensure his (and the colony's) survival. Similarly, when an ant is struggling to carry a load, other ants do not sit back and laugh, castigate, gossip, or wait for him to fail before coming to his rescue. They immediately come to the aid of the struggling ant. Do you do the same for members of your family and those who God has brought into your life? When was the last time you helped someone bear a heavy load whom you thought did not deserve help? When was the last time you collaborated with someone because you both wanted to see God do something new in the other person's life?

The third principle learned from ants is that of **preparedness**. Ants prepare for their family and for their future. Proverb 6:7-8 says that they do not have commanders, overseers or rulers, yet they store up provisions in the summer. Then the Bible asks believers what I believe to be a very embarrassing yet thought-provoking question in verse 9, "How long will you lay there, you sluggard?" How prepared are you to meet the challenges that lie ahead? If you were to become disabled, how would you live out the rest of your life? Worst still, if the Lord were to call you home today, how would your family survive economically? How prepared are you to meet your Maker?

The final principle learned from ants is that of **perseverance**. Ants are not quitters. Are you? They persevere through disturbances, danger and disaster. In other words, they are fighters who refuse to give up in spite of the circumstances they find themselves going through. Have you ever noticed a colony of ants washed away by a strong water hose? They regroup in a few minutes and refuse to be defeated. What a spirit of resilience and perseverance! Do you give in to despair and defeat easily after a few failures in life? Do you allow the enemy to discourage you when things are not going the way you anticipated?

The point that I am trying to make is that there are value principles we can learn from ants that could change our lives. It is for this reason, God says, "Go to the ants and let them teach you." In other words, examine the lives of ants; study their habits; analyze their weaknesses but also see how they make up for their weakness; evaluate their accomplishments in light of yours and ask yourself, "Am I measuring up?"

Given that there are 1,250,000 identified species of animals on earth,[4] it is a little surprising, don't you think, that God selects only a few for parables of comparison. Whatever the reason, I am convinced that those animals, to which we are compared in the Bible, have a lot that we need to learn from and as a result, we need to take the comparison seriously.

Besides the ants, the Bible compares us to eagles. In Isaiah 41:30, we read, "But they that wait upon the Lord shall renew their strength; they shall mount up with wings as eagles; they shall run and not be weary; and they shall walk and not faint."

Eagles are large birds that belong to the group of birds called raptors. The word raptor has it origin in Latin, stemming from *raptare*, meaning to seize and carry away. The Hebrew word for eagle is *Nesher*,

---

[4]   http://wiki.answers.com/Q/How_many_animal_species_ are_there_in_the_world. Retrieved April 22, 2011.

which means, "to tear with the beak." Eagles are plunderers. They, like all raptors, are predatory birds with strong, hooked bills and strong grasping feet. Eagles are some of the world's largest birds. They have excellent vision, light bodies, soaring wings and other characteristics that make them unique and peculiar.

An electronic word search of the Bible will quickly reveal that the word 'eagle' is mentioned 32 times. Bible scholars believe that in God's arithmetic, the number 32 means covenant. If the two thoughts are combined, we can logically deduce that God wants to reveal His covenant to us through the life of the eagle. God wants to use His creature, the eagle, to help us understand deep spiritual truth. The eagle therefore is another example of how God uses parables, metaphors, analogies and similes in the Bible. In His divine wisdom, God has chosen to help us see deep spiritual things through the lens of His natural creatures. What a wise God! In Romans 1:20 we read: "Ever since the creation of the world His invisible nature, namely, His eternal power and deity, has been clearly perceived in the things that have been made. So they are without excuse." The fact of the matter is that it is easier to understand spiritual truths by studying natural or earthly things. Similarly, we can gain knowledge about the 'overcoming' Christian life by looking at some of the characteristics of an eagle.

As much as I recognize that God could have chosen any bird or animal to use as a comparison, I would be very uncomfortable if God used certain animals to refer to me. Therefore, I am glad that God, in His omniscience, chose to compare us to eagles and not to any of the other approximately 10,000 species of birds that soar through the sky every day. Of course, He could have likened us to any other animal since we display some of their characteristics as well. Nevertheless, thank God, He did not do it!

For example, let me mention one creature God might have chosen to compare to humans; one of those animals that I would have been uncomfortable with God using. God could have compared us with chickens. After all, they are so common that there are probably more chickens in the world than there are people. I grew up with them living in the same house, competing for the same food (rice), tilling the same ground for survival, and running around playing in the same yard. Chickens are good animals and fun to have around. They keep the environment noisy and full of activity. The case could be made that the clucking chickens make is actually their way of talking. They sound varying alarm calls when threatened by different predators. Chickens warn one another of danger like the presence of a snake. A rooster will attack anything that he thinks will harm the hens. Their spurs (located at the back of their leg) can cause a very painful puncture wound.

Additionally, chickens are easy to maintain and can be profitable financially. Hens live five to seven years, but may live twenty years. Many hens produce eggs their entire lives, with the number decreasing as they age.

In Ancient Rome, chickens were held up as role models of motherhood, hence the Roman compliment: "You were raised by a hen," meaning you were carefully raised with good virtues and value system. Even in our day, we may call someone a "Mother hen" implying that the chicken is a good mother. It may be in reference to Matthew 23:37 where Jesus said, "Jerusalem, Jerusalem, you who kill the prophets and stone those sent to you, how often I have longed to gather your children together, as a hen gathers her chicks under her wings, and you were not willing." Certainly this metaphor speaks of the protective nature of a mother hen who reaches out to gather her chicks under her wings to shelter them and keep them safe when she believes that their lives are threatened. Chickens are very sociable animals. They also fight to protect their family and mourn when a loved one is lost.

As good and praiseworthy as some of the characteristics mentioned above are, there are other characteristics of chickens which make me thankful that God chose to compare humans with eagles instead of chickens.

First, chickens are not capable of sustained flight. The longest recorded flight of a chicken is thirteen seconds. Though chickens have large wings, they hardly use them. When threatened by a predator, chickens attempt to use their wings, but due to lack of practice, find them to be weak and mostly useless. If they resort to running, chickens are capable of traveling up to nine miles per hour by foot. Their inability to fly makes them vulnerable to predators; hence they are an easy catch.

Some situations in life require us to walk, a few require us to run but others require us to "fly." Walking at times makes it easy for us to get caught. The same is true for running. In fact, while running, there is a greater possibility of getting into serious trouble by running into obstacles, like a wall, or falling into a pit, especially when we are vigorously pursued. If we are not careful, not only will our enemies catch us, we might also sustain injuries as we try to run to safety. That is why we need to learn to "fly."

Have you noticed a plane on the runway? As it taxis before taking off, it is very vulnerable. Any little crack on the runway could cause tremendous damage to the plane. Passengers are advised to remain seated with seatbelts fastened. However, when the plane has reached a certain altitude away from relative harm, passengers are able to remove their seatbelts and enjoy the flight.

Imagine the days before planes were invented. Imagine the number of months it took a person to travel to Africa, Asia or Europe. Consider the challenges voyagers faced with waves, seasickness, vicious sea creatures, malfunctioning equipment and hurricanes. Just pondering what travelers of old endured to cover a 1,000-mile journey is scary. Today, we can simply catch a jet and "fly."

Imagine if chickens could fly. Capturing them would be difficult, requiring the use of more sophisticated methods of seizure. Unfortunately, this is not the case. When faced with vicious predators or even their human master in order to be killed and cooked, they simply surrender because they cannot fly. It is the same with many of us; we do not know how to fly away from our threatening situation. We do not know how to mount up with wings like an eagle and fly to the "Son." I hope that by the time you finish reading this book, you would have fully understood how to fly freely and never act like a chicken that is incapable of sustained flight.

Second, chickens can be hypnotized to believe they cannot leave a small space by merely holding the chicken and repeatedly drawing a circle in the dirt surrounding the chicken. Surprisingly, the chicken will remain immobile for a long period after the circle has been drawn around it, not realizing it is being fooled or hypnotized. Somehow, it does not have the ability to realize that it is being fooled or hypnotized. Whether traced by a child or adult, it allows its movements to be dictated by a simple circle.

The Bible declares that the devil is like a roaring lion looking for whom He may devour.[5] Notice that He is not a roaring lion but is like a roaring lion. To roar is to make a loud noise. A lion roars for several reasons. First, it roars to warn everyone that the "king of the jungle" is present and is speaking. The lion intends to strike fear into anyone who tries to question his authority. In other words, the enemy is instantly hypnotized and paralyzed by the terrifying roar.

At times, the Devil appears to act like a roaring lion, but you need to remember that the devil is not "The King." When the devil starts to roar at you, let the Christ who is in you begin to roar back in prayer, while standing upon the Word of God. Let the devil know that He has no right to raise his voice at you because the Christ in you is ready, willing and able to

---

[5]   I Peter 5:8

defeat him again as He did over two thousand years ago on Calvary. Simply tell him to carry his "roaring" somewhere else.

Second, a lion roars in order to paralyze his enemy, which becomes confused, frightened, and thus unable to hide. The roar's booming sound fills the air and in their state of confusion, the enemies don't know which way to run. They become completely vulnerable, and without much effort on the lion's part, they become his lunch or dinner. The devil tries the same trick on us. He roars and we think that we are going to lose our jobs, have our cars repossessed, have our home foreclosed, or worst, that we are going to die. Where is God? What has He said? Have you listened to that still, quiet voice? Can you focus on Him (Christ) and forget the noise? There is an African proverb that says, "If you pay attention to the noise in the market, you will not buy your groceries." The devil makes a lot of noise and you must not allow him hypnotize you like a chicken. If you pay attention to him, you will not walk in the promises and prosperity of God.

Third, a lion roars to scare away anyone who might attempt to interfere with the prey he has already killed. His roar is simply meant to strike fear and terror into the heart of every other creature that hears him. Isn't that interesting? The devil is somehow intimidated by the fact that you might interfere with his "catch." He has a good reason to be scared of you; for he knows the authority you have in Christ. He knows who it is that lives in you. He knows that "greater is He (Christ) who is in you than he (the devil) that is in the world." Additionally, the devil knows that when you pray and speak forth God's Word, the Father hears it and acts. That is why the devil is intimidated. He is trying to frighten you when in reality he is the one who is in a panic.

Believers need to understand that Satan's roar is nothing but a roar. He might roar in your ear to strike fear into your heart of losing your job. He might roar in your ear that you will lose your family or everything you have worked for over the years because the stock market will crash. He might roar in your ears trying to hypnotize you not to enter into that business venture that will take you from living from one paycheck to another and start living like a king. He might roar in your ear to scare you like a chicken that is hypnotized by a simple circle drawn around it and thereby thinks that if it steps outside of the circle, it would be harmed. Tell the devil that his tricks will not work on you because you are not a chicken.

You have to continuously remind yourself that even though the noise is loud, it has no substance, significance, effect or meaning because you are in Christ and His blood covers you. Unfortunately, we allow the devil to make us afraid by his roar. We think that all hell is breaking loose when the devil starts to roar in our ears. When the devil does that, it is his way of hypnotizing us into not stepping out of the cage he has placed us in. We become afraid of the unknown and forget that the Lord has given us a spirit of boldness, power, might, and a sound mind.

Have you also noticed that the Bible does not say that the devil bites; rather, it says that he roars? Simply put, he cannot bite and even if he could, God will not let him put his teeth on you. In fact, I like to envision him as a toothless being with an intimidating voice meant to frighten those who have forgotten the power they have in Christ. It is up to you to tell the devil that you are not a chicken and he cannot hypnotize you. Tell him that you have come to discover that he is not going around biting, ripping and tearing his victims to pieces because God has not given him that authority. Therefore, from this point forward, he can roar as much as he wants, scream in your ear as much as he wants, or try to hypnotize you as much as he wants, but in Jesus' name you have the authority to break his hold. In fact, begin now to take active steps to silence that voice that is paralyzing you or telling you to disobey the Lord. Silence that voice that is encouraging you to do something sinful, or is making you afraid to step out to take hold of God's promises for your life. Speak to it and command it to be quiet in Jesus' name.

You might be saying, "But you don't understand. I am really struggling and I am under serious attack. Day and night, I weep over my situation because it seems like there is no end in sight. I have tried everything that I know and have prayed all the prayers that I know." If that is your situation, then I sincerely empathize with you. I know that life can sometimes be very challenging. The devil has a way of making his roaring sound so real that we become deaf by it and nothing else seems to matter. It is true that I do not understand your situation but the magnitude of your problem does not change who God is or what His Word says. Listen to what Revelation 5:5 says: "Then one of the elders said to me, Do not weep! See, the Lion of the tribe of Judah, the Root of David, has triumphed. He is able to open the scroll and its seven seals." The Lion of the Tribe of Judah, Jesus Christ, the only begotten Son of God, made one great roar as He hung on the cross. It is that roar that is important and not the roar of the devil. When Christ roared (shouted), He declared, before giving up the ghost, "IT IS FINISHED!" It was at this moment that the veil tore and we gained access into the Holy of Holies. It was at that moment that all powers of the devil were broken and all fear, doubt, frustration, anxiety, and sin were forever placed under the Lord's feet. It is when Christ roared that we overcame the devil by the blood Christ shed and the words of our testimony. That is what our victorious

Lion (the real Lion) did for us. He is called the Lion of the Tribe of Judah.

Isaiah gives a good picture of the Lion of the Tribe of Judah in Isaiah 31:4-5:

> This is what the LORD says to me: "As a lion growls, a great lion over its prey—and though a whole band of shepherds is called together against it, it is not frightened by their shouts or disturbed by their clamor—so the LORD Almighty will come down to do battle on Mount Zion and on its heights. Like birds hovering overhead, the LORD Almighty will shield Jerusalem; he will shield it and deliver it, he will 'pass over' it and will rescue it.

Jesus is not threatened by the roaring of the devil's voice. He does not cower in fear at the sound of Satan's deceptive lies and neither should we. In Amos 1:2, we read, ". . . the Lord roars from Zion and thunders from Jerusalem; the pastures of the shepherds dry up, and the top of Carmel withers."

When the Lion of the Tribe of Judah roars, He does so from His holy mountain. Upon hearing his roar, all of creation trembles. Principalities, powers, spiritual wickedness in high places have no other option but to run in fear. Satan himself cowers in terror because our God, the Lord of Hosts, is in control and we are seated with Him in heavenly places. The Lord reigns eternal and unlimited. When His voice roars from the Throne of God—all of creation stands in attention. Angels stand in readiness to obey His commands. Demons tremble and shake. Consequently, whatever comes from the lips of God is instantly carried out, for our omnipotent Lord God has spoken. That is the roar that we should be afraid of, not that of the devil. It is the roar of God that brought the world into existence. His voice spoke, not to frighten, but to bring creation forth. When He roars, it is not to intimidate you, His child. It is not to scare you away from His presence or to make you want to hide from him. When He roars at your sickness, it is for that sickness to go! When He roars, it is for your sins to be washed away through the Blood of the Lamb! When He roars, it is to break the chains that have kept you captive for so long. Consequently, His roaring causes you to be healed, emboldened, loved, cherished, comforted, and satisfied with life.

As you read this book, ask yourself, "Which roaring am I listening to?" Are you acting like a chicken and becoming intimidated by the roar of the devil as he tries to hypnotize you and keep you from experiencing God's best for your life, or are you encouraged by the roar of the Lion of the Tribe of Judah who promises to give you life in abundance?

Allow me to take you back to the discussion on the characteristics of chickens. The third characteristic of chickens worth mentioning is that they generally follow the crowd irrespective of the motive. Chickens, attracted to energy and motion, tend to "follow the crowd" irrespective of the reason. When one chicken observes another chicken or group of chickens running, it immediately joins in with them. It probably thinks that if another chicken is running, there is a good chance it knows why and there is no need to ask but to run as well. How wrong that is! Another chicken could be running not because of danger but for the simple fact that it wants to run. Unfortunately, by so doing, it could incite lot of other chickens and thereby create a chaotic, embarrassing, unexplainable, unwarranted, and dangerous situation.

Some of us exhibit the same behavior. We tend to follow any person demonstrating zeal and energy regardless of where their leadership will take us. If we took the time to investigate the leadership we are chasing, it could save us from a lot of trouble. Additionally, just because all around you are going north, does not mean that north is the direction in which you should go. That is what a chicken does. It follows the majority.

This behavior is prevalent among young people who generally follow the crowd. They usually say, "Well, everyone is doing it, so why shouldn't I?" When will we learn to stand alone like the three Hebrew boys Shadrach, Meshach and Abednego (Daniel 3:19-30)? When will we learn to follow the Bible and not the crowd? Why do we usually want a crown without a cross and a palace without a prison? When will we stop being chickens and stop in order to analyze things for ourselves? Our friends or relatives who do not know the Lord often influence us. We see them running in a particular direction and assume that if he or she is heading that way, then that might be the way to go. Unfortunately, we sometimes do the same thing when it comes to our career. We do not make the effort to examine our options, skills, passions and desires, but simply choose a particular career path because our friends are doing so. Hope you will say to yourself or someone you love, "STOP BEING A CHICKEN! STOP FOLLOWING OTHERS AIMLESSLY! THINK FOR YOURSELF!"

Fourth, another trait of chickens is that they are known to "tiff and fight" among themselves over insignificant things. They seem to have a problem distinguishing the "tree from the forest." They struggle with knowing which battle is worth fighting and which battle should be ignored or avoided. If one chicken discovers something edible, like a bug, suddenly all the nearby chickens abandon what they were doing, and compete for that same bug. It does not matter that this very bug has been flying or walking around the yard for a long time; now that one chicken has taken possession of that bug, it has become a priced possession that all the chickens want to have. Unfortunately, the one who has possession of the bug will not let go of it easily. As a result, a marathon race begins. It becomes "survival of the fittest." Regrettably, in the end, the bug may be eaten by a different chicken that was faster or stronger. Isn't that how we are sometimes? We are often not satisfied with what we have. We always want what others have. The expression, "living like the Jones," becomes true. What we are indirectly saying to God by our actions is, "You are not blessing me enough. I want what you have given to them!" You probably do not exhibit this chicken mentality but I am sure you know someone who does. Would you please pray for that person?

Fifth, another trait of a chicken is that they are easily frightened. They are not usually good at defending themselves and since they are on the menu of about every carnivore and omnivore, they try to escape their predator by running away. In fact, one of the definitions of a chicken is a person who lacks confidence, is irresolute and wishy-washy.[6] Simply put,

---

[6] Chicken. (n.d.) The American Heritage ® DICTIONARY OF THE ENGLISH LANGUAGE, FOURTH EDITION (2003). Retrieved April 20, 2011 from http://www.thefreedictionary.com/chicken

a chicken is a coward. They run from each other, and if there is one that is aggressive, he could chase the others around the yard or chicken pen. Chickens never join forces to defend themselves against an aggressor. In addition, chickens seem to give up before even attempting challenges. If a short fence is erected, the chickens will stay behind the fence even though their wings are strong enough to easily fly them over the fence. Attempting to overcome that obstacle is not an option for the chickens. Maybe that is where we get the expression, "Don't be a chicken."

What is the last obstacle you surmounted? Have you looked the devil in the face recently and said, "I don't want to pick a fight, but if you bring it on, I am ready in Jesus' name. I am not afraid of you, for I know that my weapons are not carnal but mighty to the pulling down of strongholds?"[7] Are you easily frightened by normal challenges in life? Or do you see challenges as a stepping-stone to reach new heights in life? Chickens do not see challenges in this way but I am sure you do.

Sixth, and this is very interesting; while chickens are not able to defend themselves against outsiders or predators, there are some who are bullies. These chickens habitually steal from the others because they are bigger and more intimidating in size. These bullies

---

[7]   II Corinthians 10:5

take pleasure in showing off and do not hesitate to pick on smaller chickens. However, when attacked or approached by a larger animal or a human, they quickly back down and run. Even the roosters who usually beat on the smaller chickens are wimps. You will notice that when they are crowing in the morning and you clap your hands or stump your feet, they take off running. Since the bigger and stronger chickens are not able to defend themselves against outsiders, they feel that they have to pick on the other weaker chickens. Is that not what happens many times in life—the oppressed becomes the oppressor. Do you take out your frustration on others? Do you penalize members of your family because of what someone did to you at work? Do you ill-treat others in life because you were abused, unappreciated, or mishandled? That is what a chicken does. I am sure that you do not do that!

Finally, chickens seem to have no or little interest in things that are above their eye level. In other words, they have no interest in the heavenlies. It is true that some chickens sleep on the branches of short trees or on elevated surfaces but this is as high as a chicken would go. If they do sleep on something that is elevated, as soon as it is morning, they will jump down to the ground for the day from the elevated surface. They seem perfectly content living in the chicken yard with no vision, plan, or ambition. They have no higher aspiration than pecking the ground, hour after hour, continuing their humdrum task of scratching in the dirt for something to eat. They are always digging. I am reminded of the scripture passage which states that "an ungodly man diggeth up evil: and in his lips there is as a burning fire."[8] Most chickens never learn anything new, never venture out of their yard to explore their surroundings and never try to learn how to fly. Chickens are earthbound birds. Are you earthbound? Do you wake up thinking about the heavenlies? Do you wonder how the angels are praising the Lord on this day? Do you try to imagine the beauty and splendor of the angelic host as they worship the King of Glory? Do you think about what you could do differently to change your life? Do you wonder what life would be like were you to change your career? Are you trying to learn some new skills? What is your vision or goal in life? Where do you see yourself in the next ten years? Wow! I do not want to be earthbound! I do not want to be a chicken!

I believe that now you see and fully understand why I am grateful that God chose to compare me with an eagle instead of a chicken. In summary, chickens are not capable of sustained fight. They are wimps. They cannot resist the onslaught of an enemy.

---

8   Proverb 16:27 (KJV)

Beloved, please learn from chickens how NOT to live. Do not be like them. In Jesus name, you have to be able to resist the plans of the wicked one. Obviously the devil would like to make you believe something different from what the Word of God has said concerning you. The devil wants to hypnotize you exactly as chickens are hypnotized. You cannot afford to be like chickens. You need to know who you are and whose you are. You have been bought by the blood of the Lamb and filled with His Spirit. Paul said, "I can do all things through Christ who gives me strength" (Philippians 4:13). No one should have the power over your destiny but God. No one should be able to stop you from moving forward but God. No one should be able to halt or abort what God has destined in your life but Him. You must refuse to be hypnotized by anyone or anything. Your mind ought not to be controlled by anyone or anything but by the Spirit of God. That way you must not follow the crowd like chickens do. The crowd will mislead you and take you to a place where God did not intend for you to be. I am reminded of the saying, "sin will take you farther than you want to go, keep you longer than you want to stay, and cost you more than you want to pay."[9]

No doubt, even if you do not agree with the reasons why I am grateful to God for not comparing me with a chicken, I am sure that you at least agree with me

---

[9] Author unknown

that living the life of a chicken is not God's best for you. In fact, it is nothing close to what God originally designed for you. From the beginning of creation, the Bible declares that God made man in His image, in the image of God He created him, male and female He created them. Then God blessed them, and God said to them, "Be fruitful and multiply; fill the earth and subdue it; have dominion over the fish of the sea, over the birds of the air, and over every living thing that moves on the earth."[10] Do you realize that when God made man and woman, the first thing they heard was His blessing of them? Blessing means to release favor and benefit. This is God's desire. He wants to bestow His blessings upon our lives. It may not necessarily be financial blessings but it could be spiritual, emotional, psychological or other forms of blessings. In fact, in Ephesians 1:3 we read, "Praise be to the God and Father of our Lord Jesus Christ, who has blessed us in the heavenly realms with every spiritual blessing in Christ."

God's original intent was not for us to be like chickens but to be like eagles. This sums up the heart of God to us all. He wants to bless us! Chicken living is so limited, so confining, so predictable, and so boring. However, living the life of an eagle—that is another story! Now you can see why it is so important for you to stop living like a chicken. Denounce your

---

[10] Genesis 1:27-28

"chickenly" lifestyle and start living like an eagle. When you understand how to rise up and live like an eagle, you will understand one of the great mysteries of the Christian faith. People will look at you and marvel. You will no longer be content with living with mediocrity, but will start living a dynamic, victorious and overcoming Christian life. You will start mounting up and riding on winds effortlessly. You will remember that victory is your portion. You will claim goodness and mercy as your companions. You will tell the devil "enough is enough." God made you for the heavens and no one can stop you!

CHAPTER II

UNDERSTANDING THE ANATOMY
OF AN EAGLE

"Their faces looked like this:
Each of the four had the face of a human being,
and on the right side each had the face of a lion,
and on the left the face of an ox;
each also had the face of an eagle" (Ezekiel 1:10).

In order to fully understand why God compares us to eagles and not to chickens, it might be helpful to examine some of the skills, talents or abilities of an eagle. Hopefully so doing, we will not only come to fully appreciate God's wisdom and divine enlightenment, but we will realize all that He has bestowed upon us, in comparison to eagles and we will therefore get busy living as eagle Christians. The best place to begin our quest to understand the skills, talents and abilities of eagles is in examining its anatomy (physical structure). The physical features of an eagle permit it to perform feats that most birds could only dream of, but would never even come even close to accomplishing in their lifetime.

Before that though, let me ask you this simple question: What comes to mind when you hear the word, 'eagle'? For me, I picture a bird soaring in the atmosphere, effortlessly riding the wind currents high above the earth. I think about a bird that is king of the sky and master of his domain. I consider a bird that is beautiful and majestic in appearance. I wonder in awe at a bird that, when it spies its prey, swoops down with tremendous speed, snatches the prey with its sharp strong talons and soars back to its nest leaving onlookers baffled at its rapidity, dynamism, and accuracy. Perhaps it is for these very reasons that nations, kingdoms, and empires for centuries have recognized the eagle as "king of the birds" and have had its proud image reproduced on their coins, seals, emblems and flags.

You may already be aware that there are approximately 59 different species of eagles found all around the world and on every continent, with the exception of Antarctica. These various species of eagles have been placed into four principle groups: the Sea or Fist Eagles, the Snake Eagles, the Harpy Eagles, and the Booted Eagles.[11] In spite of their differences, all eagles are predators

---

[11]   htttp://www.indiana.edu/~bradwood/eagles/what.htm. Retrieved May 8, 2011

or raptors and they are highly admired and respected. Across all cultures, the eagle is perceived to be a large, beautiful, noble, and powerful bird that symbolizes power, justice, courage, freedom, and immortality. Its grandeur has inspired mankind for generations even as it still does today. In 1782 the United States adopted as its central motif on the Presidential seal a spread-winged bald eagle brandishing the arrows of war and the olive branch of peace to represent the strength and liberty of the nation.[12] Similarly, on the national seal of Mexico an eagle is pictured devouring a serpent, symbolizing the triumph of good over evil. It is worth noting that eagles are used not only as symbols within the geo-political arena but within religious circles as well. Many ancient religions viewed the eagle as symbolic of the divine and protective strength of the deities and they were believed to be companions of chief gods. In Hebrew and Christian traditions, the eagle represents the flight of the soul to heaven and the fulfillment of the messianic promise. Since the eagle soars upward, it symbolizes the resurrection and ascension of our Lord Jesus Christ. When an eagle has a halo, it is symbolic of John the Evangelist, because of his lofty and "soaring" gospel.

Although the eagle is considered by many to be the "king of the sky," it is interesting to note that the eagle is not the largest flying bird. Though most eagles are

---

[12] http://hubpages.com/hub/eagle-bird. Retrieved, May 10, 2011

large and powerful hunters, it may surprise you to learn that some eagles, such as the crested serpent eagles, are as small as chickens. Some eagles fly short distances, eat insects and even fruits but they are still eagles. The crested serpent eagle is so named because it may spend all day in an African forest searching for snakes. Did you get that? It looks for snakes to eat! The very animal, which terrifies other birds and causes them to flee, is exactly what a crested serpent eagle chooses for its prey. It is not afraid of snakes and does not stop for one second to consider the snake's size or whether it is poisonous. It knows what it has; what it is made of; who made it; and what it has done to other animals it has caught for food. The question is, what does an eagle have? What is it made of? Better still, since God compares us to eagles, then the question is, what do we have? What are we made of? Let us examine the anatomy of an eagle, compare it to ours (spiritually) and hopefully, we will see why the Lord chose to compare us with eagles.

First, let us consider the weight and strength of an eagle. An eagle weighs between twelve and twenty pounds, but what is impressive is that an eagle is able to lift and carry away prey up to three times its size. That could be like a person who weighs one hundred pounds, lifting and carrying a three hundred pound individual for over 10 miles. This sounds impossible to believe, but it is true. When full grown, an eagle can lift a medium-sized deer weighing between 65 to 90 pounds.[13] It is believed that the eagle's superior strength can be attributed to its diet. In other words, eagles choose wisely the things they eat (healthy diet). Eagles feed on freshly killed prey and shy away from eating anything that is already dead or that they personally did not kill. Although eagles have a voracious appetite, they are wise not to eat every part of the animal they kill because their systems do not easily digest body parts like bones and hair. These indigestible items would just sit in the eagle's craw, weigh the bird down, and impair the ability of the eagle to fly freely. If an eagle accidentally eats a bone or the hair of its prey, it attempts to rid itself of those unwanted objects that have entered its system. In order to rid itself of these items and resume its flight unhindered, the eagle would hit its beak against a rock for as long as it would take until whatever it has consumed is expelled. As painful as this process may be, the eagle does not hesitate to do so because the consequence of allowing the unwanted objects to remain could be deadly. Unlike the eagle, hyenas and vultures routinely feed on dead carcasses. They even pick through the "leftover" carcass remains other animals have already fed from. Disturbingly, they do not know when to stop eating, leading to bodily injury from overeating. As a result, they become intoxicated

---

[13] http://wiki.answers.com/Q/How_much_weight_can_a_bald_eagle_lift. Retrieved, May 10, 2011

from the dead carcass or over-engorged and can neither move nor fly. This vulnerable state sets them up to become prey for other animals.

The same is true for us as believers in regards to our weight and strength. We need to be physically fit. Many times believers quote Zachariah 4:6[14] as an excuse to be lazy. We eat anything we lay our hands on and sometimes find it hard to pray because we are so full with food that our spirit man finds it difficult to stay in tune with the Spirit of God. There are times that God wants to speak to us during the "cool of the day" but we are so lazy that we will not get up from our slumber or find the time to go somewhere in order to sit in the presence of the Lord and allow His Spirit to minister to us.

It is disturbing to contemplate the fact that if we continue to allow "junk food" into our bodies, refuse to regulate our diet, and omit exercising, we will soon discover sickness waiting for us at our doorstep. It has been overwhelmingly documented by medical experts that many health challenges are closely associated with being overweight and eating an unhealthy diet. Obesity is a cosmetic problem as well as a health dilemma. It contributes to heart disease and stroke,

---

[14] So he said to me, "This is the word of the LORD to Zerubbabel: 'Not by might nor by power, but by my Spirit,' says the LORD Almighty.

high blood pressure, diabetes, gallbladder disease and gallstones, gout, osteoarthritis, breathing problems such as sleep apnea and asthma, and the list goes on and on. How can you pray for at least two hours as Jesus asked his disciples to do when you can hardly stand or walk? How can you "wrestle with God" in prayer like Jacob when you cannot stay awake? How can you fast (abstain from food) for a certain period of time when all you think about is food? By the way, do you know what kind of food is not good for you, and do you stay away from it? An eagle knows what is harmful to eat, and if it is consumed accidentally, the eagle expels it from its system immediately. How do you expel unwanted food? Do you exercise regularly?

That being said, we may not be as physically strong as God would want us to be, either due to laziness, a debilitating medical condition, or simply because of the aging process. Actually, an abundance of physical strength might not be required to accomplish what God has destined for us to do. The major challenge many of us face is not the lack of physical strength but our inability or unwillingness to utilize fully our God-given abilities. You might be wondering exactly what I mean. Let me illustrate. How many people do you know who are utilizing all of their body's functions to their fullest capacity? It is stated, though not scientifically proven, that an average human does not use more than 10 percent of his/her brain capacity. William Shakespeare wrote in Hamlet, "What a piece of work is a man! How noble in reason! How infinite in faculty, in apprehension how like a god!" When asked by J. Hawes of Huntington Beach, California, "What is the memory capacity of the human brain? Is there a physical limit to the amount of information it can store?" Paul Reber, Professor of Psychology at Northwestern University, replied:

The human brain consists of about one billion neurons. Each neuron forms about 1,000 connections to other neurons, amounting to more than a trillion connections. If each neuron could only help store a single memory, running out of space would be a problem. You might have only a few gigabytes of storage space, similar to the space in an iPod or a USB flash drive. Yet neurons combine so that each one helps with many memories at a time, exponentially increasing the brain's memory storage capacity to something closer to around 2.5 petabytes (or a million gigabytes). For comparison, if your brain worked like a digital video recorder in a television, 2.5 petabytes would be enough to hold three million hours of TV shows. You would have to leave the TV running continuously for more than 300 years to use up all that storage.[15]

---

[15] http://www.scientificamerican.com/article.cfm?id=what-is-the-memory-capacity, Retrieved September 16, 2011.

The point is that we overlook what we have and often time, do not even utilize what we have. If each of us would start using a fourth of our brain capacity, imagine what our world would be like. God has already given us what we need physically. Our anatomy was designed by its Maker to accomplish the seemingly impossible. As time goes by, we observe new technology and inventions others have created, and we are amazed. Humans, like ourselves, are accomplishing these wonderful things, and yet we allow the devil to persuade us that we are good for nothing and do not have what it takes. We must stop listening to the lies of the devil and rise up to our true identity. God has blessed us in many ways. Start using what you have and rely on the strength of the Lord. The psalmist declares, "The LORD is my rock, my fortress and my deliverer; my God is my rock, in whom I take refuge, my shield and the horn of my salvation, my stronghold."[16]

The same is true spiritually. God has given us the ability to be spiritually strong. The Bible declares, "For though we live in the world, we do not wage war as the world does. The weapons we fight with are not the weapons of the world. On the contrary, they have divine power to demolish strongholds."[17] Because Christ lives in us, we have been clothed

---

[16]   Psalms 18:2
[17]   II Corinthians 10:3-4

with His authority to fight in His name and He has guaranteed that victory will be ours for the taking. It is for this reason that He told Jeremiah, "See, today, I appoint you over nations and kingdoms to uproot and tear down, to destroy and overthrow, to build and to plant."[18] Obviously, Jeremiah could not do this in his own strength, but with God's help, he realized that all things were possible.

I am sure you have read or heard about a man named Gideon (Judges 6:1-8:35). He was not a hero from the very beginning. As a matter of fact, he was actually a timid farmer who did not typify courage and strength. In Judges 6: 11, we read that the Lord's angelic messenger came and sat down under the oak tree in Ophrah owned by Joash the Abiezrite. He arrived while Joash's son, Gideon, was threshing wheat in a winepress so he could hide it from the Midianites. He was a discouraged man filled with bitterness, fear, doubt and timidity. However, when he encountered the mighty God and realized that he was made to act like an eagle and not a chicken, his outlook on life changed dramatically. The farmer, who earlier described himself as the least in all of Israel, now saw himself as God saw him: a hero, a military giant, a warrior, a brilliant orator, a motivator, a conqueror, a diplomat, and a servant of the living God. Gideon's life changed when he consciously decided to believe God

---

[18] Jeremiah 1:10

and take Him at His word. He refused to feed on dead news. He refused to believe the lies of the enemy. He refused to allow himself to continue to be humiliated. Instead, he chose to look into the heavens where he could find the throne of God. He chose to focus on the God of the impossible. He chose to learn how to fly as an eagle, knowing that he was destined to lead and not to hide or to be led. He understood that when you hide, you would one day be discovered and pulled out of your hole and humiliated by your enemy. He understood that some things must be faced head-on. He understood that some things are worth fighting for even if it means fighting until death. That is what an eagle does. However, in order to do so, it must be physically fit. That is why the eagle cannot afford to overeat or consume what is unhealthy.

The same is true for us. If we want to be healthy spiritually and face our enemy, we must not consume dead things. In other words, we must stop the gossiping, cursing, slandering, drinking, filthy jokes, and begin to take in the Word of God. We need to read what God's Word says and listen to what His Spirit is speaking to our heart because that is what determines our strength. It determines who we are or who we will become. It is precisely for this reason that we need to guard the three gates through which we take things into our body; namely, the eye, the ear, and the mouth. We need to be extremely careful about what we allow our eyes to see. If we are looking at pornography, x-rated movies and other things that will defile our mind, then we will continue to act like chickens. In the same manner, we need to be selective of what we allow our ears to hear. We cannot claim we want to live like eagles if we constantly allow ourselves to be bombarded with stories of defeat, frustration, discouragement, fear, and heartbreak. The Bible asserts that without faith, it is impossible to please God.[19] But, the faith we need to please God comes by hearing.[20] It is therefore imperative that we do not allow ourselves to hear negative things about God and about others. Sometimes we have to be honest and tell others, "Thanks for wanting to share the news but I do not need to hear it." Of similar importance, we need to be mindful of what we take in through our mouth. In other words, we need to watch what we eat both spiritually and physically.

Proverbs 18:21, instructs that life and death are in the power of the tongue, and those who love it will eat of its fruit. Therefore, we ought to be careful that no evil talk comes out of our mouth. Some things simply make us fat and lazy. They sit on our chest, like dead bones in our craw, and we cannot pray, sing, run or rejoice in the Holy Spirit. Some of us cannot even walk seven times around our "Jericho wall." Consequently,

---

[19] Hebrews 11:6
[20] Romans 10:17

"flying" becomes an impossible task. Like unwise birds, we take in what harms us, and by holding on to it, we are hindered from flying, and thus we set ourselves up to be vulnerable to the enemy's attack. We need to intentionally and persistently get rid of them as the eagle does. We need to confess our sins and ask God for forgiveness. In some cases, we might need to make restitution (if possible), while in other cases, we may need to humbly ask our loved ones to show us loving-kindness, tender mercy and forgiveness. The point is if we are going to fly as eagles, we must put aside every sin that easily besets us. The writer of the book of Hebrews says, "Therefore, since we are surrounded by such a great cloud of witnesses, let us throw off everything that hinders and the sin that so easily entangles, and let us run with perseverance the race marked out for us."[21]

Another important feature of the eagle is its eyesight. Eagles have the reputation of possessing the sharpest eyes in the sky and its vision is believed to be at least four times stronger than a human with perfect vision. An eagle's excellent eyesight permits it to spy a rabbit almost a mile away; something that a human is unable to do without the aid of binoculars.

It is worth mentioning that the eagle's eyes and head are not larger in size in comparison to the

---

[21] Hebrews 12:1

human eyes and head. However, their eyes do seem to be larger in proportion to the size of their head especially when one looks at the size of a human eye and a human head. Therefore, one cannot argue that because they have big heads and eyes in comparison to humans that is why they have better eyesight than humans. Their ability to see farther can be attributed to a number of things.

First, an eagle's excellent eyesight is due in part to the dual-focus areas in each eye. An eagle has both binocular and monocular visions. The former permits the eagle to see forward, and the latter allows it to see out the side or slightly backwards. The combined capacities permit the eagle to see small objects that are far away.

Second, an eagle's eye has a different shape than that of a human. The back of an eagle eye is flatter and larger in comparison to that of a human eye. This helps to enlarge the image that the eagle sees.

Third, the retina in an eagle's eye has an increased number of concentrated rod and cone cells, which are responsible to send sight information to the brain. For an individual who has perfect vision, he may have in his fovea approximately 200,000 cones per millimeter. For an eagle, there may be approximately one million cones per millimeter, which is believed to be the same number of visual cells found in the monitor of the best computer in 2011 when set at its highest resolution.22

Fourth, an eagle, like many other birds, has three eyelids—the bottom, the top and the inner eyelid. The bottom eyelid is bigger than the top and, therefore, an eagle blinks up instead of down as we do. Its inner eyelid, called the nictitating membrane, is also used for blinking but it slides across the eye from front to back. The nictitating membrane wipes dust and dirt away from the cornea, allowing the eagle to see without any obstruction. Since the nictitating membrane is translucent, the eagle is able to see even while it is covering the eye.

Fifth, eagles, like all birds, see in color. The vision of humans is based on three basic colors, whereas eagles have superior color vision utilizing five basic colors. This further differentiation enables an eagle to see preys that are well camouflaged.

You may be wondering what this has to do with us as believers and why this ability of an eagle to see farther should interest us. Let me point out that even though God did not provide us with as good physical eyesight as an eagle, He has made available to believers "spiritual eyesight" which is much more valuable than

---

[22] http://www.learner.org/jnorth/tm/eagle/VisionA. html#Eyes. Retrieved May 19, 2011.

physical eyesight. I wear glasses because I do not have a 20/20 vision. In other words, my eyesight is not very good. In fact, I am near-sighted. It means that I do not see things that are far away. I struggle to recognize small objects or signs that are a few feet away from me. I have been praying for a miracle but God has not granted me one yet in regards to my physical vision. Maybe, He is saying to me, as He said to Paul, "My grace is sufficient for you, for my power is made perfect in weakness."[23] Even with that assurance, I do admit that it is a struggle at times for me. How I wish everything about me was perfect. How I wish I had the best vision there is plus more. How I wish I did not have to wear glasses every morning before leaving my house. How I wish I could see the beauty of the world all around me without an artificial aid. Unfortunately, that is not the case. And although I do not hold God responsible for my situation, I can honestly say like Paul, "Therefore I will boast all the more gladly about my weaknesses, so that Christ's power may rest on me." It is the power of the spiritual vision Christ gives that is most important. Some people have good physical vision but cannot really see what they ought to see. They see only with the limitations of their physical eyes. They see only on the surface but not deep into the heart. Some people lack the vision to see beneath the surface at others' motives. Their faulty vision notices the outward smile, but

---

[23] 2 Corinthians 12:9a

cannot see the cruel intent of the heart. They see only the beautiful face, but miss seeing the malicious and vindictive plans underneath, planning their demise.

From my experience in life and ministry, there are three kinds of people you will find in your life: **destiny killers, destiny helpers and destiny fulfillers**. The challenge for us as believers is that many times we confuse the three. It is in this area that we need to pray for divine insight or spiritual eyes as keen as an eagle. Destiny killers are people who you trust, who you call confidant and confide in, and whom you love dearly. Destiny killers may be those you call friends and with whom you share the same meal, and who you think are looking out for your interest. However, they are the very ones who will betray you, insult you, use you, mistreat you, and "suck up your blood" like a leech, a mosquito, or even worse, a vampire. Then when they are done harming you, they dump you, walk on you, and leave you to rot. You know what I am talking about, do you not? Those are destiny killers. Their goal is to learn where you are headed, and then conspire with your enemies to set an ambush for you. Their sole intent is to hinder you from getting to your destination. They appear to be good but they are evil personified.

Recently, my wife and I were at a conference where a minister expressed her disappointment in the way some church folks have treated her. As she expressed her hurt, many of us in the room quietly identified with her plight. After she recounted her story, another pastor said, "God has called us to love His people dearly, but we need to learn how to hold them lightly. He continued, "If we don't pray and ask God to show us the difference and learn how to walk in wisdom, we will soon realize that in loving them dearly and holding them firmly and closely, we could get hurt deeply." What a profound revelation! Perhaps you may not completely agree with the pastor's statement but you have to agree that there is a measure of truth in it. When God expands your vision to be able to see in the spiritual realm like an eagle has expanded vision to see in the physical, you will be able to distinguish the destiny killer from the destiny helper and destiny fulfiller.

The second group of people we find in our lives is the destiny helpers. These people help facilitate a segment of our journey on the way to our destiny. God may not have ordained them to accompany us all the way to our destiny, but they do play a pivotal role, which is in some way significant. Their assigned role may be to assist us through our first years of college, marriage, child bearing, or other transitional period.

When this phase of our life passes, they too may fade out of our life.

I recall when I was planning to come to the United States in 1998 to study at Bethany College of Missions in Bloomington, Minnesota. I had received my I-20 and had made an appointment to go to the embassy for an interview to get my visa. It was around that time that the U.S. Embassy was bombed in Kenya. All (or almost all) of the U.S. embassies were closed around Africa. Additionally, part of the agreement with the school was that I would come to the United States with my entire family. I was almost certain the embassy would not grant us the visas. I did not have the required amount of money in my bank account and worse, I did not have a sponsor. It was beyond my wildest imagination how I was going to get the visas for my family of four! The Sunday after I received my I-20, I was scheduled to preach at church. While preaching, I noticed (I saw as an eagle sees) a black tall man entering the church. He quietly sat at the back of the church and listened attentively to the preaching of God's uncompromising Word. When the worship service ended, the guest came to greet me, and in his jogging outfit, and with a huge smile on his face, he introduced himself as "Mr. Brown." He mentioned that he was blessed by the sermon and wanted to sit and talk with me. Upon looking at him, I asked myself, "What kind of man will come to church in a jogging suit?" How dare he enter

God's house without taking a shower and with sweat dripping all over him after doing his exercises. I said to him, "I am deeply sorry but I cannot. I have another appointment this evening." I was not lying. I did have another appointment but even if I did not, I was not sure if I wanted to meet with him. He seemed deeply disappointed. He bowed his head, turned around and started walking towards the exit. I felt sorry to disappoint him, but I was not ready to compromise what I thought to be a basic dress code for those coming to worship in the house of the Lord. Suddenly, as though someone turned him around as if he was a robot, I saw him quickly turn and start heading back towards me. I said to myself, "Now what!" I must add that though I had just come from ministering under the anointing the Holy Spirit, I was not sensitive to what the Lord was doing. In fact, I have noticed over the years of preaching that when I have completed delivering God's Word with the demonstration of the Holy Spirit's power and anointing and I descend from the pulpit, that is when I am the least attentive to what the Lord is saying either in my spirit or through others. I immediately enter into an "analytical mode" where I begin to review what happened during the service and question if I missed anything God wanted me to do. In any case, Mr. Brown came straight to me in spite of my initial rejection to meet with him and said, "Here is my business card, in case you change your mind." I thanked him politely and with a fake smile, I accepted the card even though I was saying to myself, "There is no way that I am going to change my mind." I placed the card in my pocket and on my way home, I felt a prompting in my spirit to look at it. When I did, I noticed Mr. Brown was a senior diplomat and a former U.S. Ambassador to the Ivory Coast. It goes without saying that my schedule immediately cleared, my attitude changed, and I was on the phone with him setting up the appointment for us to meet that evening. Thank God for His grace. In answer to prayer, God had supernaturally sent Mr. Brown to help me get the visas for my entire family so we could come to the United States, and I was not operating in the Spirit to know what the Lord was doing. In fact, I almost threw away the opportunity the Lord had arranged. In three days, we had our visas even though the visa section of the U.S. Embassy remained closed to the public. My family was given the royal treatment during the entire process; even receiving a military escort to the embassy. Once we arrived in the United States, I attempted to contact Mr. Brown to thank him, but all the numbers we were given had been disconnected. To this day, we have not seen, heard from or heard about Mr. Brown albeit all the effort we have made using modern technology and social networking. I believe with all my heart that Mr. Brown was a destiny helper. I could have missed out on what God was doing had He not supernaturally opened my eyes to look at Mr. Brown's card to see with the eyes of an eagle that it was an angelic or supernatural visit. What if I had thrown the card through the window or discarded it immediately after he handed it to me? Only heaven knows what would have happened. Oh, that God will help us to see what He is doing on our behalf. It is no wonder the Word of God declares in I Corinthians 2:9, " . . . No eye has seen, no ear has heard, no mind has conceived what God has prepared for those who love him." If only we knew or could see . . . what a difference it would make!

Those who were ordained to be our destiny fulfillers are the ones who travel with us all the way and take us into our promise land. Your destiny fulfillers are those folks who will stay with you through thick and thin. They will not leave no matter what the situation. God has ordained and anointed them to take you into your destiny. These are the people who will not leave you just because you made a mistake or because life has dealt you a crippling blow. Your destiny fulfillers are the ones who will cry with you, laugh with you, eat dry bread with you, invest their last cent into you, fight with you but will never, ever leave you. Do not get me wrong; destiny fulfillers can be a "pain in the neck." They will look you in the face and tell you when you are messing up. They will sound angry and at times yell because they love you and do not want you to be destroyed. They will warn you of impending danger because they want you to stay safe. But, no matter what they say or do, or how you perceive their rebukes, corrections, or friendship, they are not going anywhere. They are with you for the long haul. Their destiny is tied with yours. Their success is connected with yours. Their service to the Lord and others is connected with yours. They understand that the relationship that exists between the two of you is a "God thing." You are meant to be connected and no amount of demons in hell will break that connection no matter how hard they try. Consequently, they will give everything they have to see you succeed. These kinds of people are rare, precious and extremely hard to find. When you find one or two, your life and ministry will never be the same.

I am reminded of the story of Ruth. In spite of Naomi's insistence, Ruth refused to leave Naomi and return to her people. Ruth remained steadfast in her determination to go with her mother-in-law. This determination caused her to say, "Don't urge me to leave you or to turn back from you. Where you go I will go, and where you stay I will stay. Your people will be my people and your God my God. Where you die I will die, and there I will be buried. May the LORD deal with me, be it ever so severely, if even death separates you and me."[24]

---

[24] Ruth 1:16-17

That is commitment! That is what it means when someone says, "I have your back covered." They will correct you in love (if they have to) but they will stay with you. Pray that the Lord will send those "destiny fulfillers" into your life.

It is extremely important to understand that even though we constantly encounter these three kinds of people in our lives, we must be extremely mindful of the first category, those who are destiny killers. After first praying, when the Lord opens your eyes to see as an eagle and you find out that someone is a destiny killer, you need to swiftly disconnect yourself from that individual. People like that are chickens. You cannot afford to hang out with them. They will take you down into the pit with them. Since they are earthly focused, they will cause you to take your eyes off the heavens and begin to concentrate on the petty things of life. They become excess baggage, nightmares and discouragers. In fact, they become stumbling blocks to your progress, and the only thing that you can do is to stop associating with them or else they will start to stink and pollute your house, environment, and life. They will stink so much that others will not want to come around you because of the smell. You may think that you are doing them a favor for old time's sake by keeping them around, but in reality you are hurting yourself and the vision the Lord has given to you. If they continue to hang around you, your chances of reaching your destiny will be greatly reduced, if not destroyed. Conversely, when God opens our eyes to see those who are our destiny helpers, we need to love, appreciate and cherish them while they are with us. However, we need to know that they are with us but for a short time. Any attempt on our part to make them stay longer then they have been destined, will prove to be very disappointing and even disastrous. A man of God likened them to those who get on the bus. If you are the bus driver, you should be content with the fact that some people will get on and off while you are driving the bus. They will occupy space, strike up good conversation, help you avoid an accident, tell jokes to help make the journey fun and enjoyable and more than anything else, they will contribute financially by purchasing their tickets for the ride. Some of them will even be generous enough to give you a tip, write you a lovely note or send you a gift on your birthday or during the Christmas season. But you, as the driver of the bus, need to remember that when it is time for them to disembark from the bus, you need to stop the bus and let them off. Failure to stop and let them off when requested could change the atmosphere in the bus from being friendly to becoming violent. You, as the driver, and other passengers aboard the bus could sustain verbal or bodily harm in extreme cases from the one who appeared to be so nice and friendly just a few minutes ago. In other words, when it is time for them to go, let them go. When they want to visit other churches, let them visit. When they want to hang around others and ignore you, let them do so. When they feel that it is time to walk away from the friendship, let them do it without any contention or fight. They have served their time and purpose. Accept it and move on! God will bring more people to occupy the bus. He will never allow your bus to remain empty and even if He does allow it to be empty physically, it shall never be empty spiritually because the Father, Son and Holy Spirit will always be there with you. When you feel abandoned or neglected, you need to realize that God will never abandon you. In fact, you need to realize that where some people are getting off your bus, others are usually getting on. Our challenge is to see those who are getting on and value their presence. Seldom do you see and appreciate others after a painful breakup, or neglect. Our mind remains connected to the person who left and we grieve for the love or relationship that is no more. Sometimes we have dreams and we fantasize about their returning when we know in reality, they have moved on. Sometimes we keep their pictures to remember those beautiful times we spent together when we know that the pictures could serve as obstacles to our starting new and promising relationships with others. We sometimes even go as far as taking their names to a witch doctor to place a spell on them in order for them to return to us. Look, you are better than that! If the relationship is dead and you did everything you could to keep it alive but it still died, move on. You have done your best. That person probably did not deserve you. Refocus your attention on what is alive and not on what is already dead. Remember, an eagle does not eat an animal that it found already dead. You need to see that God has not and will not abandon you. You need to see what God is doing in the supernatural. You need to see that if one destiny helper disembarks, God has many more that He will bring onto the bus. You cannot afford to sit and grieve over the ones who have left. If they left you, it means they were not destined to go with you all the way. It means they were not destined to see the Promised Land with you. Some are meant to die in the desert while others are meant to cross over into the promise land. That is why an eagle does not eat an animal that it found dead. The eagle does not know what caused the animal's death; perhaps it had a contagious disease. That is why it looks for animals that are alive. You need to stop looking for dead things. If a relationship is dead, "kill it!" You might challenge me saying, "What do you mean? How do I kill something that is already dead?" You can do so by disconnecting yourself from whatever emotion still exists in your heart for that person who is "dead." You can ask the Lord to help you get rid of the emotional pain, hurt, frustration or even fun memories that you had with that person. You can bury those feelings and never return to them. Do not get me wrong. I am not trying to be insensitive. Yes, it is okay to grieve. Grieve if you must, but get over it quickly. Cry when the relationship dies but bury it quickly before the foul odor contaminates you. Some people still hold onto a love that no longer exists. If a man or woman (boy or girl) left you for someone else, then move on! Sitting and crying forever or trying to commit suicide will not solve the problem. Complaining will not bring the person back. Becoming depressed will only create a medical situation that you do not want or worsen an already existing medical condition. You need to see and appreciate those who are there to help you fulfill a task or to go through a portion of your journey. Bid them farewell and God's speed when it is time for them to get off the bus. Do not try to hold them back. You have been a destiny helper for some people as well. I am sure that you have let others down and gotten off their bus. It is not the first time and it certainly will not be the last time either.

Pray that God will give you the eyes of an eagle to see beyond your natural abilities. When Jesus walked on the earth, He spoke in parables. When asked by His disciples why He spoke in parables, Jesus replied: "Because the knowledge of the secrets of the kingdom of heaven has been given to you, but not to them . . . . . Though seeing, they do not see; though hearing, they do not hear or understand"[25] Speaking of "not seeing,"

---

[25] Matthew 13:11-13

Elisha's servant could not see how God was going to deliver Elisha and him from the surrounding armies of the King of Aram. All He could see were enemy chariots and horses. Elisha prayed that God would open his servant's eyes to see that those who were for them were more than those who were against them. The Bibles declares that the Lord opened the servant's eyes, and he looked and saw the hills full of horses and chariots of fire all around the walled city.[26] That is what I call having spiritual eagle eyes; eyes that see into the spiritual realm. God has made this special eyesight available for all who seek after Him. If He opened the eyes of Elisha's servant in the days of old, He can still do it today. Hebrews 13:8 says that He is the same God yesterday, today and forever.

The third characteristic of an eagle's anatomy worth mentioning is its beak. The beak of an eagle is large and conspicuous, usually as long as the eagle's head. The primary purpose of the beak is to tear apart and kill the prey. In other words, the beak is a weapon that finishes what the talons began. Given the fact that an eagle does not chew its food, the beak enables it to tear the food into smaller, bite-sized pieces before consuming it.

An eagle's beak is comparable to the mouth of a human. Though they do not look the same and they

---

[26] II Kings 6:16-17

function a little differently, the beak of an eagle and the mouth of a human have some similarities. First, both serve as the means by which food enters the body for consumption. Second, both are used to break the food into smaller pieces for consumption. Third, both serve as one of the channels through which communication takes place. Even though eagles do not have vocal cords like humans, they still produce sound in the syrinx (a bony chamber located where the trachea divides to go to the lungs). The call eagles produce warns nearby predatory animals that the territory within the hearing of that call is the eagle's hunting zone, and he is prepared to vigorously defend this territory from all other hunting animals. Stay away or you will pay the price. Additionally, the eagle's call reinforces the bond existing between the male and the female eagle mating pair, in the same way that conversation between married couples reinforces trust. The fourth aspect to consider about an eagle's mouth is the shape of the beak. Usually the beak serves as a vital and powerful part of the eagle's body. Without it, an eagle will find it difficult, if not impossible to survive. However, because of its unique shape, it can (rarely) cause the eagle to become trapped or entangled when trying to reach its prey. Thus, the beak may cause the eagle to become entrapped and himself become a prey for other predators.

The same is true for the mouth of a human. It is useful for communication, consumption of food and pronouncement of blessing. However, the mouth can become an instrument of entrapment. We hear the expression continuously; "he shot himself in the foot." That is what happens when you misspeak or when your mouth gets you into trouble. Unintentionally, your mouth entraps you at times. In the Bible, the word "mouth" is used interchangeably at times with the word "tongue." Solomon is quoted in Proverbs 18:21, "The tongue has the power of life and death, and those who love it will eat its fruit." We also read in Proverbs 12:18, "The words of the reckless pierce like swords, but the tongue of the wise brings healing." In other words, within our mouth lies the power of life and death. The words we utter can pierce like a sword or they can heal. What we say to one another has the ability to affect us more often than we care to admit. Sometimes, words can and do hurt more than sticks and stones. We often utter words that we regret deeply but unfortunately, we cannot withdraw them. Once a word or expression has been recklessly uttered, there is nothing that we can do but regret what has been said. The book of Proverbs gives many ways in which we use our words recklessly. They include, gossiping, lying, deceiving others, speaking in anger, speaking selfishly or prideful, complaining, using foul language, swearing, or cursing.

Instead of focusing on the negative ways and stating how we can use our mouth to dishonor the Lord and others, allow me to share a few ways we can learn to control our mouths. The first lesson is to learn how to "bite your tongue." I do not mean to literally bite your tongue. I am suggesting that you restrain yourself from blurting out the first thing that comes to mind. The mind has a way of playing a nasty trick on us. Sometimes the first thing that comes to mind may not necessarily be what is needed to bring about healing and reconciliation. On the contrary, it could be exactly what the enemy wants you to say in order to sow strife, resentment, confusion, hatred, and hurt. Unfortunately, we fall into the devil's trap and please him by verbalizing the thought that he brought to our mind. Then, he sits back and watches us make fools of ourselves, belittle the name of Christ and call into reproach the testimony that we have spent years trying to build as believers. Sometimes your intention may be good but it could be misunderstood or misinterpreted. Many times your good intentions are not even taken into consideration. A comment you meant to be humorously sarcastic instead deeply cuts into someone's already existing wound and causes it to start bleeding afresh.

Controlling your mouth is therefore vital. In Proverbs 21:23 we read, "He who guards his mouth and his tongue keeps himself from calamity." Oh how true that is. I have gotten into a lot of trouble when I have not been able to bite my tongue. That may not be your challenge, but I am sure you know of someone who needs prayer in this area. At times, we talk a little too much. Proverbs 10:19 warns, "When words are many, sin is not absent, but he who holds his tongue is wise." Paul wrote to the church in Ephesus, "Do not let any unwholesome talk come out of your mouths, but only what is helpful for building others up according to their needs."[27]

The second way to control your mouth is to think before you speak. It is obvious that if you do not blurt out the first thing that comes to your mind, then you will learn to think through the situation before speaking. The same book of Proverbs says that the heart of the righteous weighs its answers, but the mouth of the wicked gushes evil.[28] Given the shape of an eagle's beak and the fact that its hooked tip could be caught on something, an eagle is very careful not to stick its beak into a hole. It would rather give up and seek new prey than to persevere after an animal hiding in a hole through which the eagle's entire body cannot fit. How I hope we could learn from the eagle! The principle is simply, "Don't try to put your head where your body cannot fit." Rephrased, one would say, "Don't hang your hat where your hands can't reach." Or, "Don't

---

[27] Ephesians 4:29
[28] Proverbs 15:28

pick a fight that you know you cannot win." Obviously, the ideal situation is not to pick a fight in the first place. When we learn to control our mouths and think before we speak, we will ask ourselves ahead of time, "Will my words or comments help or hurt?" "How can I say it in a better way?" The proverb many of us heard from our parents is applicable in this situation; "If you cannot say it nicely, do not say it at all."

The third lesson we need to apply when controlling our mouth is to learn to listen before we speak. This is extremely hard for some people especially when they strongly disagree with what someone is saying. Sometimes you know that the person is dead wrong about what he or she is saying or has completely deviated from the core issue being discussed. It takes the grace of God to continue listening respectfully. But, don't we need the grace of God in every situation? I think we do, and especially in controlling our mouths. Solomon once noted that the one who answers before listening, "That is his folly and shame."[29] Is it not true that in certain situations, we are more interested in making our reply to a statement than in listening to and comprehending the original statement? How often do you take the time to rephrase what you have heard and ask for clarification? How many times have you not listened carefully, taken someone's words out of context,

---

[29] Proverbs 18:13

become angry at what you thought they said, only to find out later that you were completely mistaken? James admonished the church in these words which are applicable to us today as well: "My dear brothers and sisters, take note of this: Everyone should be quick to listen, slow to speak and slow to become angry.[30] If we listen carefully before speaking, we will not fall into the trap of: a) planning our answer before the other person is done speaking; b) engaging in selective listening and responding harshly; c) reaching a verdict in our mind before a thorough conversation; d) leaving unsaid details that would have drastically changed the outcome. I am of the strong conviction that if we are truly looking out for the interest of others, we will listen more than we talk. Someone once said, "God is wise. He gave us two ears and one mouth for the purpose of listening more and talking less." Paul wrote to the church in Philippi and cautioned them not to do anything out of selfish ambition or vain conceit, but in humility they should consider others better than themselves. He further admonished each of them to look out not only for their own interests, but also for the interests of others."[31] If listening before you speak is a challenge for you, allow me to suggest a technique that could change your life forever: withhold your opinion in a conversation unless someone asks for

---

[30] James 1:19
[31] Philippians 2:3-4

it. While withholding your opinion, pray quietly for the person who is speaking. I know that it is difficult, but with God's help, it is possible and you can do it. What a difference that would make!

Lastly, one of the best ways to control your mouth is to pray before you speak. Obviously, it would be illogical and unrealistic for me to suggest that you always remain quiet or withhold your opinion in every conversation. However, in the case where you feel an urgent desire to speak, be quick to ask the Holy Spirit to help you utter the right words. In Colossians 4:6 we read, "Let your conversation be always full of grace, seasoned with salt, so that you may know how to answer everyone." Our words can be "seasoned with salt" if they are first and foremost encouraging. Proverbs 12:25b states that an encouraging word cheers a person up. Additionally, our words are "seasoned with salt" when they are kind and gentle when responding to others even if what they are saying to us is hurtful. Proverbs 15:1 says that a gentle answer turns away wrath, but a harsh word stirs up anger. Not responding in the same harsh tone we have received does not in any way demonstrate that we are weak. On the contrary, it shows that we are strong and are above "petty quarrels." In fact, one of the fruits of the spirit is meekness, which simply means, "strength under control." A meek person certainly feels the injustice done against him. However, because the meek individual understands the heart of God, he will not allow that unjust situation to give rise to hateful and vindictive rage, with the goal of getting even. He would instead feel pity for the perpetrator's poor judgment and his other character flaws. Consequently, the meek person, rather than using his mouth to inflict harm, will cry out as Jesus did in Luke 23:34, "Father, forgive them, for they do not know what they do." With a mindset of seeking the interest of others and wanting to honor Christ always, the aggrieved party who is meek, tempers his or her reaction and allows the love of Christ to be manifested.

Finally, let me add that the key to controlling your mouth is guarding your heart. Jesus told his disciples in Luke 6:45, "The good man brings good things out of the good stored up in his heart, and the evil man brings evil things out of the evil stored up in his heart. For out of the overflow of his heart his mouth speaks." In other words, your mouth speaks what is embedded in your hearts. It simply means that if you allow God to transform and control your heart, then your mouth will be fine also. When your heart begins to reflect the heart of Christ for others, your mouth will begin to confess His will for them as well. It will come without a struggle.

I have discussed significant comparisons between the anatomy of eagles and the anatomy of humans and why God chose to compare us to eagles, and I am sure you have gotten the point. If not, simply find a picture of an eagle, examine it closely, and ask God to open the eyes of your understanding, and I can assure you that you will be amazed by what you will discover. But, let me mention one final thing before ending this chapter.

When you take a close look at the picture of an eagle, you will probably notice the shape of its feet. In comparison to other birds, an eagle has powerful feet, which allow it to capture and kill its prey easily. An eagle's feet are usually large and its talons are menacingly long. They are backed by tremendous muscular force from the eagle's legs, enabling the eagle's talons to easily penetrate and, in some instances, crush the bones of its prey. An eagle "locks" its prey in the grip of its talons by contracting its muscles, allowing the tendons in the lower legs to tighten and close together. This locking system allows an eagle to hold its prey steady, even while the eagle is at rest or falls asleep. The eagle also has under its fleshy toes sharp, prick-like spikes called spicules, which assist the eagle to grasp and hold onto slippery prey such as fish. I am reminded of what God said to Joshua when Moses His servant died. He said in Joshua 1:2-6:

Moses my servant is dead. Now then, you and all these people, get ready to cross the Jordan River into the land I am about to give to them—to the Israelites. *I will give you every place where you set your foot,* as I promised Moses. Your territory will extend from the desert to Lebanon, and from the great river, the Euphrates—all the Hittite country—to the Mediterranean Sea in the west. No one will be able to stand against you all the days of your life. As I was with Moses, so I will be with you; I will never leave you nor forsake you. Be strong and courageous, because you will lead these people to inherit the land I swore to their ancestors to give them."

"What an amazing creature with an almost flawless anatomy," one could say! God has indeed made a creature that has astounding characteristics and body features. However, it would be wrong and unforgivable were I not to point out that the eagle has challenges with parts of its anatomy just as we do with ours. In as much as it is true that the eagle has excellent weight and strength, impeccable eyesight, mastery over its beak, and incredible feet, there are other parts of the eagle's body that are less impressive. For example, the eagle's sense of hearing is only comparable to that of a human being's and its sense of smell is not nearly as impressive as its eyesight. Similarly, the eagle's sense of taste is less developed. In other words, the eagle has some of the same challenges and limitations as we have.

What is important is that an eagle does not focus on its weaknesses, but rather capitalize on its strengths and use them to become the master among the birds that fly in the sky. An eagle does not pity itself, bemoaning the less-than-perfect parts of its body. Rather, it soars high up into the sky and enjoys life to the fullness, as God destined. I do not know about you, but I have been caught many times comparing myself with others, wondering why I am not as handsome as this person or as brilliant and creative as another. Sometimes I have wondered if I could ever accomplish much in this life given all of my limitations. Maybe I am alone, but somehow I am sure that others sometimes find themselves in the same situation . . . . just wondering. I must say that when I find myself in that situation, God, in His kindness, reminds me of the gifts, skills or abilities He has given to me. He has a way of "opening the eyes of my understanding" to see beyond my prevailing situation and help me recognize how far He has taken me from where I used to be. Truly, He has already done amazing things in my life. He has a way of helping me count my blessings, naming them one by one. He has a way of letting His Spirit speak to my spirit man and remind me that I am not where I want to be, but I am not even in close proximity to where I used to be. He has a way of reminding me that He has given me all that I need to live a victorious and prosperous life. And then, He finally speaks to me those comforting words: "I am not done with you yet. Give me a few more weeks, months, years and you will be amazed." When I hear Him speak like that to me, I become encouraged because I am His child, and He is working things out for me. I remind myself that I do not need to live up to someone else's standards; I am who I am because of the grace of God and I have been wonderfully made by Him. I remind myself that God is faithful and He will see me through in His own time and in His own way.

What a God we serve! We have some deficiencies but God has given us what we need to get the job done and bring glory to His name. Like the eagle, we need to learn to wait. "For they that wait upon the Lord, shall renew their strength . . ." (Isaiah 40:31). Sometimes the eagle has to wait. It has to wait for the right moment. The moment has to be God designed, God appointed, God planned, and God executed. When that time comes, you will know. An eagle knows. It has the instinct to know when it is time to mount to the skies. The eagle does not run ahead of the wind; but waits until the moment is right. You too, do not run ahead of God! You may encounter challenge, but God will perfect your situation in due season. Wait, trust, pray and you will see what He will do!

Chapter III

Understanding a Few Mysteries

"There are three things that are too amazing for me,
four that I do not understand:
the way of an eagle in the sky,
the way of a snake on a rock,
the way of a ship on the high seas,
and the way of a man with a young woman"
(Proverbs 30:18-19).

The passage mentioned above is intriguing and mystifying. The writer says that he is flabbergasted by the following: One, the ways of an eagle in the sky; two, the way of a snake on a rock; three, the way of a ship on the high seas; and four, the way of a man with a young woman. Do you find these four facts easy to comprehend? Notice also that the writer's statement implies that these things are so intrinsically interesting that it is difficult to explain all of the activities related to them. He uses the word, "amazing," which could mean that these things are so wonderful to him that he is never tired of watching them while at the same time lacks the words or understanding to explain them. The first, he says, is the way of an eagle in the sky. Wow!

I must admit that I struggled to understand the true meaning of this passage and quite honestly, I am not sure if I fully understand it. However, let me begin this chapter by telling you what I do understand about these four mysteries because they are connected to the life of an eagle and subsequently, ours as well.

One can understand and try to interpret these mysteries both naturally and spiritually. When we try to interpret them naturally, they leave us scratching our heads because of their complexity and for the mere fact that they are "mysteries." However, when we try to interpret them within a spiritual context, especially in light of Christ's love for the church, His body, we will then be able to see the wisdom and revelation contained in this passage and start to praise the Lord for His goodness. Let us examine them in reverse order.

Naturally, "the way of a man with a young woman" speaks of love, affection, care and the deep sense of appreciation he has for her. A man and a young woman "mysteriously" fall in love with each other and together, make the decision to be joined in holy matrimony. Certainly, what is described here is not a forced or arranged marriage as is customary in some societies. Yet, all of us will agree that when an older man falls in love with a young woman, this love should be guided, controlled, and tamed or else it could lead to abuse, abandonment, adultery, frustration, hurt, hatred and sometimes even to an untimely death.

For the sake of clarity, I do not believe that the Bible is referring to a few years (one to five years) difference between a man and a woman (or a girl). As a matter of fact, it was acceptable in biblical times for an older man to marry a young girl as in the case of Joseph and Mary (the mother of our Lord Jesus Christ). Even today, many psychiatrists advocate the acceptability for an older male to marry a younger female. Dr. LouAnn Brizendine, a Neuropsychiatrist who has written about brain development in males and females, believes that girls' brains mature as much as two years ahead of boys' during puberty and it is possible that boys may not catch up to girls until late adolescence or when they are in their early twenties. Consequently, she argues, a few years between partners does make a compatible match.[32] I think the gap in age between a marital couple becomes an issue in our culture today when it is significantly wide or when it violates established laws or cultural norms. Yet, it must be noted that some young women are

---

[32] http://abcnews.go.com/2020/story?id=2504460&page=1. Retrieved on December 12, 2011.

attracted to older men for various reasons. Let us look at three of those many reasons.

First, a younger woman may be attracted to an older man because of stability. Most women look for stability in a man whether emotional, financial, or social. Most young women do not want a man who is unsettled and has not found a secure path for his life. Given that most older men are stable in their jobs, have decided to settle down, have survived financial storms, have endured diverse experiences and have successfully weathered various life challenges, they bring a wealth of experience to the relationship and it makes the younger woman more comfortable.

Second, some younger women prefer entering a relationship with an older man because they are generally disciplined, responsible, dependable, caring, loving and affectionate towards them. The older man's affection could be natural or out of fear that his mate will go out to find someone of her age and fall in love with him. Be it as it may, he usually showers her with love (attention, flowers, gifts, money, etc). He continues to wine and dine her even as he continues to make her feel like a princess, his valued treasure, his pride and joy.

Third, an older man may exude an air of maturity, meeting the emotional or psychological need of a young woman for fatherly figure in her life. Many women admire their fathers and wish that their husbands would exhibit some of the characteristics found in their fathers. Some did not have the opportunity to have their dads present in their lives. Hence, for them, marrying an older man brings a sense of security, admiration, protection, love, longevity, and peace to their lives. The husband becomes either the father that this woman had always admired or the father she had longed to have but was not present in her life. Logically then, marrying an older male makes a lot of sense for some young women no matter what society says or what the views of their relatives or close associates.

Having given at least three reasons why some younger women are generally attracted to older men, it is worth mentioning that there are some serious consequences which may affect the couple with a great gap in their ages. Some of these consequences are so serious that it may become unacceptable, even a crime in some cases, for an older man to become sexually involved or married to a younger woman.

The first factor that I have already alluded to is the age factor. Some societies have set a minimum age limit for marriage. Though it varies from one country to another, it is generally set at age 18. Some countries allow marriage to take place at a slightly younger age with parental and or judicial approval, or in case of pregnancy. Fifty-five countries are parties to the Convention on Consent of Marriage, Minimum Age for Marriage, and Registration of Marriages,[33] which requires them to state the minimum marriage age by statute law, thus overriding customary religious and tribal laws. It is therefore safe to say that there is a general consensus (especially in many Western Countries) that the love an older man has for a younger girl should be regulated.

The second reason why some societies frown on an older man getting married to younger girls is her lack of psychological maturity. Some psychiatrists believe that girls are not fully mature until they reach at least the age of seventeen. Girls seventeen and younger tend to act impulsively, relying heavily on peer pressure in their decision-making. This may cause a girl to make a hasty, unwise relationship decision. Adolescents are convinced they know what is good for them and that they are able to differentiate between right and wrong. Yet, because of their psychological immaturity, they may not fully understand the

---

[33] The treaty was opened for signature and ratification by General Assembly resolution 1763 A (XVII) on 7 November 1962 and entered into force 9 December 1964 by exchange of letters, in accordance with article 6. The Convention has been signed by 16 countries and there are 55 parties to the Convention. http://treaties.un.org/pages/ViewDetails.aspx?src=TREATY&mtdsg_no=XVI-3&chapter=16&lang=en. Retrieved December 12, 2011.

devastating consequences such major life's decisions could have on them in the future. In other words, a teenager's ability to carefully, calmly and analytically examine a matter is somewhat limited in comparison to adults.

The third and final reason to be wary of a wide age gap between an older man and a young woman is that of domination or power struggle. The older man may have the advantage of power over the young woman who is innocent and ignorant of his strategies. Her lack of experience in life may limit her in knowing how to respond to him and some of the challenges they face in their marriage. Additionally, she may not be able to say "no" or defend herself when she disagrees with him. It may lead to her being bullied or intimidated into doing or accepting things simply because she does not know how to or lacks the experience in dealing with some pertinent issues in life. Consequently, she may feel trapped and eventually become frustrated, depressed, and miserable. If the situation is not dealt with immediately, it could lead to divorce, medical emergency, or even death.

Recently, I had a conversation with a young woman who is a believer and a divorcee. She was married to a man who was about two decades older than she was. She explained that she had a tendency to be attracted to older men. Although she initially thought it unwise to marry a man about twice her age, she eventually fell in love with this older man who made her feel safe, treasured and loved. Unfortunately, their marriage ended because the husband became overly protective and jealous. He felt extremely insecure and his jealousy turned into an obsession. "Love" became "hate" and life became unbearable. She was monitored constantly, followed wherever she went, and her phone was tapped. Though she loved him dearly, she became afraid for her life, wondering what terrible thing he would do to her if she were caught innocently talking to a male associate. She finally became convinced that if she were caught talking to another man, her husband would kill her. In fact, after numerous threats on her life, she had to escape and thus ended the marriage.

I am not sure what your theological views are concerning whether she should have left the marriage or not. However, the point that I am trying to make is that, in as much as, there are many good reasons why a younger woman is attracted to older men, there are some risks as well. It is therefore easy to see the reasons why this issue is controversial in many societies. Many may argue even further that it is an emotional, psychological, physical and cultural mystery why older men fall in love with younger girls and vice versa, because many times the risk is not worth the benefits. Some mention the likelihood that the older husband will eventually become a medical liability and possibly die years before the younger woman, leaving her a widow in the prime of her life. Others warn that the older husband may become unable to sexually fulfill his marital responsibility, and the younger woman could become tempted by other men, and thus defile her marital bed. This is a debate that started a long time ago and it is not my hope to provide a permanent solution in this book. That is why the writer of Proverb 30:18-19 describes the way of a man with a woman as a mystery.

Let me quickly point out that a young female eagle does not go looking for an older male eagle that is about the age of her father to establish a mating relationship. She looks for youthfulness, strength, agility, fertility, wisdom, and his ability to provide for a family. Now, do not get me wrong. I am not in any way suggesting that younger women should not marry older men because we do have examples in the Bible of older men marrying younger women. It is even believed that Jesus' mother, Mary, married Joseph, a man believed to be much older than she was. Additionally, the Bible provides no specific guidelines stipulating the age differences that may be appropriate in order for marriage to occur between a man and a woman. However, it could be argued that there are inferences in Scripture that one should marry someone of one's own age group. For example, it is difficult to believe that the lovers described in the Song of Solomon had a wide age disparity between them. In fact, we read in Proverbs 5:18, "Let your fountain be blessed, and rejoice with the wife of your youth." Do you not think that the writer is referring to a young man and a young woman in this passage? That is certainly my belief.

However, the point is, the marriage of an older person to a much younger one may not be the norm (especially in our culture) but it does happen, and more importantly, Scripture does not seem to forbid it. Hence, it would be inappropriate for us to forbid it on Christian grounds, especially where the union does not contradict the laws of the land. I think what is most important is the reason(s) for wanting to enter into such a relationship. What is the motive of the younger person wanting to marry the older one and vice versa? Marriage is a covenant that should not be broken. Entering into such a union for the wrong reason is diabolical and could have devastating consequences. Wrong motives can come from the man or woman; the parent; the younger or older suitor. A selfish parent may want a daughter to marry an older man with wealth or prestige. A younger woman may be what we call in America a "gold digger." Meaning, when the old man dies, the young widow goes and digs up his gold (wealth or treasures).

We need to guard our hearts. We are cautioned in Proverbs 4:23, "Above all else, guard your heart, for it is the well spring of life." In Proverbs 14:30, the Bible declares that a heart at peace gives life to the body but envy rots the bones. When one gets married for the wrong reason, it becomes a disastrous recipe for sorrow, regret, frustration and a troubled heart. It robs you of your joy, peace and happiness. It saps your energy and takes away your youthfulness. It allows the enemy a hold on your life and suppresses your dreams for a better future. It cheats you of the friendship and mutual respect that should exists in the relationship. It enables the enemy to accuse you of being selfish in the presence of God. It breaks your heart, leaves you in a state of confusion, and abandons you to rot. I hope someone reading this book will get the revelation found in Luke 12:15, "Then he said to them, 'watch out!' Be on your guard against all kinds of greed; a man's life does not consist in the abundance of his possessions." Do not get married because of the "things" that the other person possesses. The anointing upon your life as a child of God should not be compromised because of worldly possessions. We are told in Deuteronomy 8:18, "But remember the Lord your God, for it is He who gives you the ability to produce wealth, and so confirms His covenant, which He swore to your forefathers, as it is today." As a covenant child, God's anointing is upon your life and that anointing can produce whatever it is that you need to live this life. That anointing is able to break the yoke of poverty, grant you favor, increase your barns, give you the intelligence you need, open doors that no man can close, and miraculously provide the husband you have envisioned. Keep in mind that God has deposited in you what it takes to be a good wife or husband and you can also trust Him to attract the person He has destined for you.

I recall many years ago when I saw my wife and fell in love with her. She did not think that I was the one for her. She decided that she did not want to spend the rest of her life with a guy like me. I was really a "loser" at the time in every sense of the word. I am not sure if I am not still a "loser" (but it is for you to judge). Anyway, in all honesty, I probably would not have wanted to marry myself. I did not even want to date myself. I knew that I was not ready for dating and I was definitely not ready for marriage. I considered myself a disgrace to "manhood". I did not have a cent in the bank, was unknown, not established in any particular career, running away from God's calling like Jonah in the Bible, and worse, I was a refugee living in a foreign land with no hope for a better future. I lived in a room along with two other friends; all three of us crammed into a space only 20 feet long by 15 feet wide. We could not afford to pay our monthly rent of approximately $35 at the time. Talk about being a loser! How much worse could it get! I definitely could not afford to eat every day and often had to resort to begging to put food in my stomach. Prior to my refugee experience, when my future wife and I knew each other in Liberia (our country of birth), she actually did not like me and could not stand to be in my presence. But, I can truthfully report to you today that our marriage is one of the best on the face of the earth. The grace and anointing of the Lord upon my life attracted her and brought her to the point where she could not resist me any longer. I remained persistent and trusted the Lord. She agreed to marry me when I did not have a saving or checking account. She agreed to marry me when I probably did not have more than five trousers and shirts to wear. But you see, I believed what the Lord said in Proverbs 18:22, "He who finds a wife finds a good thing and obtains favor from the Lord." I knew that my destiny was tied to hers. I knew that if I wanted additional favor from the Lord, I needed to marry her. I knew that when I got married, doors would open that were initially shut. I knew that when we got married, together we would be able to put ten thousand to flight. I knew that when we got married, her presence would take me to places that I could not go before.

Thank God that He brought to pass everything I believed. When we got married, I received a full scholarship from the U.N. to study at the University in Cote d'Ivoire. A "full scholarship" meant it covered everything: rent, transportation, books, school fees, plus allowance. Together, we later opened several businesses, employing Ivorians and those from other nations. The favor of God multiplied because we obeyed God.

My testimony is unique to me. I am not suggesting that a man should propose to a woman and put her through the same hardships my wife suffered. I am merely describing how I combined hard work with belief in the Word of God concerning our situation. I did not leave any stone unturned. I did whatever was necessary to take care of my wife. More than once, I walked 12 miles each way to deliver my resume to offices in search of a job or scholarship to take care of my wife. The point I want to make is—let God direct your steps! When He does, you can be assured that it will be well with you. I feel a strong anointing upon my life now as I write this portion of the book. I want to declare to you prophetically under the anointing of the Lord that in the past you may have been refused, rejected, passed over, looked down upon, but I declare to you that as you read this book, today is your day; this year is your year. What the enemy meant for evil, the Lord is turning it around for your good. The problem you are experiencing now, you will see no more. What God has in store for you, the enemy cannot and will not steal from you, in Jesus' name. If you are trusting in the Lord for a spouse, tell the Lord that you will not marry for the wrong reasons. Tell Him that you will look up to Him for the one He has for you. Tell Him that you are confident that the anointing He has placed upon your life is more than enough to attract your spouse. Make a vow to Him affirming your refusal to engage in any activity that is contrary to His Word. End by thanking Him and resting in His presence.

I plan to include testimonies in my next book regarding this portion of the book. I know God will do something spectacular in the lives of those who are reading this book and have prayed this prayer believing that it will surely happen in their situation. Wow! God is good! Anyway, let us return to the passage being studied.

From a spiritual perspective, the Proverbs passage relating to the way of a man towards a young woman could be interpreted to be describing the relationship that exists between Christ and His bride, the Church. In her ignorance and innocence, Christ loves her dearly and He will do everything He can to protect, preserve and present her faultless to the Father. Christ's love for His church (the bride, us) is not selfish, self-seeking, self-centered, abusive, and controlling. On the contrary, it is liberating, empowering, enriching, and fulfilling. His love is unending, encircling, penetrating, indwelling and refreshing. It reminds me of the song, "Jesus love is very wonderful . . . . It's so high you can't get over it; So low you can't get under it; So wide you can't get round it; Oh, wonderful love!"

The other mystery mentioned in Proverbs 30:18-19, "The way of a ship on the high seas," can be understood in light of the fact that there is no beaten track or worn course on the ocean highway, yet the ship cuts through the surface and then the waves roll over its path, completely eliminating any trace. In other words, the ship has no track to follow; yet it finds its way. Similarly, the water erases its track after it passes. Just looking at a ship on the vast sea, it is impossible to determine its destination. You have to be onboard and or acquainted with ship's itinerary in order to know where it is headed. In other words, a ship does not sail aimlessly. It is headed somewhere and in spite of the vastness of the sea and its mystifying nature, the ship is built to survive and its captain is not afraid. Additionally, the captain is not perplexed by what he sees. On the contrary, he has a compass and a destination in mind. The ride may be bumpy, uncertain, cloudy, rainy, and dark; yet, the captain of the ship remains focused on the destination. That is the mystery!

Life, at times, is like riding in a ship on a high sea. Notice, the passage does not simply talk about a ship on a sea. Rather, it says, a ship on a high sea. A high sea is generally considered to be the open seas of the world outside the territorial waters of any given nation. It is important to also point out that ships sailing the high seas are expected to abide by the maritime rules of the State whose flag the ship is flying. However, if the ship or its occupants are involved in criminal activities, like piracy and illegal smuggling of drugs, the maritime law called universal jurisdiction allows any nation to exercise jurisdiction over the ship or its occupants when they are caught.

Let me share three things that I deduced from the analogy of the ship. The first is that a ship sailing on high seas ought to be mindful and stay on course. The captain is charged with the responsibility to ensure that the ship stays on course, and for this he consults the compass. When the captain confirms his course to the reading of the compass, the ship in most instances reaches its destination without any major incident. The same is true with us. God has given us His Word and it has the ability to guide us through difficult and uncertain times. The psalmist said in Psalms 119:105, "Thy word is a lamp unto my feet and a light unto my path." The challenge that many of us have is that we become less cautious at times and allow ourselves to drift away from the Word. It happens because of what I like to refer to as the five D's:

a) Depth—(Matthew 13:5-7, 20-21)—Settling for a shallow relationship with Christ.
b) Denial –(Mark 14:10-11)—Refusing to admit who we are and whose we are.
c) Difficulties—(Galatians 4:8-11)—Caving under life's pressures and challenges.
d) Deception—(Galatians 1:6-9)—Being swayed by the enemy or false doctrine.
e) Division—(Galatians 2:11-12)—Succumbing to disunity, envy, and jealousy.

The devil continually tries to influence us to drift away from God but we must, like the sea captain, grab onto our compass and stay the course. Life is full of twists and turns but ultimately, if we keep our hands in the hands of the Master, He will take us to where He wants us to be.

Second, because of the possibility of attack, a ship sailing in high seas needs to be protected from pirates and dangerous creatures that live in the sea. The devil is the Christian's number one enemy. He does not like us because we belong to Jesus. We look like Jesus, talk like Jesus, act like Jesus, behave like Jesus, minister to others like Jesus, preach the Word like Jesus, and depopulate the devil's kingdom like Jesus. That is why he does not like us. Additionally, we no longer belong to the devil and have turned our backs on him. Jesus is now Lord of our lives and the devil does not like that. Even those of you who are not busy preaching, talking, and acting like Jesus, the devil still doesn't like you because you have the Lord's ownership on your forehead (Revelation 9:4). Therefore, he attacks you constantly. His goal is to weaken your faith in order for you to turn away from the Lord. Jesus said to Simon in Luke 22:31, "Simon, Simon, Satan has asked to test all of you as a farmer sifts his wheat. I have prayed that you will not lose your faith" (NCV).

When your faith is under attack, there are a few things you need to remember. The first is, trust in Jesus more than you trust in your emotions. When a ship is on the high seas and the wind is blowing and the tide is high, the captain cooperates with the ship. He trusts the ability of the ship to withstand the weather and the compass to lead even in the midst of intense obscurity. Second, cooperate with God. Christ's comparison of Simon's test to a farmer sifting wheat pointed to the positive outcome of the process. When a ship is on high sea, and the wind is blowing, and the tide is high, the captain cooperates with the ship. He does not physically fight against the wind. He allows the ship to sail. He allows the wind to propel the ship forward. That is exactly what an eagle does. It mounts up upon the wind and soars. It does not fight against the natural wind currents but uses them. The wind is a force created by God or allowed by Him and we must recognize its place in our lives. If we understand how it works, we can benefit from it. The great inventor, Thomas Edison, failed for over three years attempting approximately 250 times to make an electric light bulb. Many years later a reporter asked him how he found the motivation to keep going after so many failures. "I guess I never considered them failures," Edison replied. "I just found a lot of things that did not work." Consider the trials of your faith to be a rite of passage necessary for you to pass into a higher state of blessing. James says in James 1:2-4, "Dear brothers and sisters, whenever trouble comes your way, let it be an opportunity for joy. For when your faith is tested, your endurance has a chance to grow. So let it grow, for when your endurance is fully developed, you will be strong in character and ready for anything" (NLT). Third, when your faith is being tested, take the focus off yourself. This may be hard, but that is what Jesus instructed Simon to do. He said, "Help your brothers be stronger when you come back to me." The job of the captain of the ship is not only to steer the ship but also to ensure that everyone on the ship makes it to his or her destination safely and peacefully (as much as possible). Hence, he cannot focus on his own fear or worries. He has to be strong for the many passengers onboard the ship. The same is true for us. Others are watching us. If we are shipwrecked, many will go down with us. Many lives are depending on us. We cannot afford to sink our ship in high seas. Finally, when our faith is being tested, we need to relax knowing that Jesus is praying for us. Romans 8:34 says that the Lord Jesus Christ, who died and was raised to life, is seated at the right hand of the Father, making intercession for us. If Jesus is praying for me, I do not need to worry. If Jesus is praying for me, I do not need to be afraid of what the future holds. If Jesus is praying for me, then I know that my life will come to an expected end. If Jesus is praying for me, no demon in hell can withstand me. If Jesus is praying for me, then all of heaven is on my side. If Jesus is praying for me, then I can sleep well knowing that He is taking care of "business." I do not know about you, but just the thought that Jesus is praying for me is more than enough for me. Because He is praying for me, I know that my ship will not sink and even if it does, there will be a lifeboat waiting to take me to shore. The mystery is solved and I have nothing to worry about!

Third, a ship that intends to sail on high seas ought to be equipped to withstand the unpredictable weather and uncertainty associated with sailing long distances with no land in sight. As Christians, we have an enemy that is ruthless and cunning. Every day, he executes carefully crafted plans aimed at our destruction. Throughout the centuries, he has launched countless attacks aimed at crippling the Church of Christ. There are at least four strategies that Satan employs in his attack against us (the bride of Christ) while we sail on high seas. He tries to:

- ❖ Disarm us—to strip us of our power.
- ❖ Distract us—to divert us from our purpose.
- ❖ Disable us—to impair our productivity.
- ❖ Destroy us—to completely neutralize our potential.

II Corinthians 2:11 states, "We are not ignorant of his devices." He comes to steal, kill and destroy (John 10:10). His desire is to see us sink our ship and never rise up again. But, he is late. Jesus made provision for our victory and has given us what we need to overcome the evil one. We are protected because of the blood He shed on the Cross of Calvary on our behalf. Consequently, the Bible reminds us in II Corinthians 10:4 that the weapons we fight with are not the weapons of the world. On the contrary, they have divine power to demolish spiritual strongholds.

If you are wondering what weapons we have at our disposal as Eagle Christians, let me name a few based on II Chronicles 20, the story of King Jehoshaphat. In this story, the king was faced with a serious crisis. His "ship" was about to sink. Three nations were poised to attack Judah and Jerusalem. His initial reaction was to panic, but then he remembered the Lord, used the weapons God provided, and experienced victory. The weapons he used were:

A. **Prayer**: He declared a time of prayer and fasting (20:3-12). He reminded God of His past deliverance (verses 6-7), appealed to Scripture (verses 8-9), presented the problem to the Lord (verses 10-11), and then he placed the entire situation in the Lord's hands.

B) **Proclamation of the Word of God**: He proclaimed the Word of the Lord to the People (20:13-17). One of our greatest tools in spiritual warfare is the Word of God. Jesus used the Word when He was under attack and Satan wanted to sink His ship.

C) **Praise**: He and the children of God praised the Lord (verses 18-19).

    i.   We should praise the Lord **before** the battle or before our ship starts to sink on the high seas. Notice that they started to praise the Lord as soon as they heard the message from the Lord's prophet.

    ii. We should praise the Lord **during** the battle. Jehoshaphat appointed singers who went before the army and they praised the Lord.

    iii. We should praise the Lord **after** the victory is won. After God gave them the anticipated victory, the people assembled in the Valley of Berachah to praise the Lord for what He had done for them (verse 26) and again in

> Jerusalem with harps, lyres and trumpets (verses 27-28).

From a broader spiritual perspective, the mystery of the ship sailing on the high seas portrays the body of Christ, the Church, surviving in the midst of sin and the sea of wicked humanity. Jesus declared that the gates of hell would not prevail against His church.[34] Like any ship, the church is headed somewhere. A ship may seem to be sailing aimlessly, but make no mistake, the captain of our Ship is taking us somewhere and He is in control. Just as a ship is built with the awareness that it will encounter difficult conditions on the sea, the Church is aware that it will encounter troubles, trials, and tribulations. Just as a ship's crew is prepared and knows what to do in bad weather, the same is applicable and true about the Church. Before Jesus ascended to heaven, He told His disciples, "I have told you these things, so that in me you may have peace. In this world you will have trouble. But take heart! I have overcome the world."[35] Spiritually, it is a wonder how the church has survived the worst onslaughts of the devil over the years. The old Negro spiritual says, "Even the angels wondered how I got over." There are times when the devil unleashes his host of demonic forces against us. We are bombarded from every side. A storm turns into a hurricane and

---

[34] Matthew 16:18
[35] John 16:33

then a tsunami without any advance warning. There seems to be no place to hide or run because the roof is gone and the building is falling apart. The only hope and consolation we have is that we are anchored to our sure foundation, Christ, the solid rock. It is baffling when we sometimes walk away without even a bruise.

This confused the psalmist! Like the ship, we appear to be directionless, hopeless and aimless, yet, we have a focus and a destination in mind. Moreover, the Holy Spirit, the "WIND of God," takes us through and though we walk through the "valley of the shadow of death, we fear no evil." I feel like jumping and praising the Lord! Can you not see evidence of the power of God at work? Can you not see what He has done for you? Can you not see how He has led you over the years? Can you not see how He provided a "way of escape" when you were entrapped? Always remember—the enemy thought you were useless, fruitless, barren, crippled, broken, crushed, and destroyed; that it was just a matter of time before you would be buried for good. But God had another plan. He had something else in mind. Before the foundation of the world, He knew that He was going to establish you and reveal unto you the riches of darkness that are hidden in secret places.[36] Give God some praise! The devil will never understand. Some things were not meant for him to understand. What matters is the fact that God knows

---

[36]   Isaiah 45:3

the plans He has for you and He will bring them to pass.

The third mystery that the proverb writer describes in this passage is "the way of a snake on the rock." We know from observing nature that a snake will creep out of a dark, cool cranny, and bask on a hot rock, warmed by the sun. When it hears an intruder advancing, it darts into another fissure. It therefore becomes difficult to trace the snake. No one knows where it came from and certainly it becomes difficult, if not impossible, to know where it is headed. Just watching the movement of a snake is mysterious in and of itself. It has hundreds of vertebrae and ribs. Their ventral rectangular scales found underneath the snake correspond directly with the number of ribs. The bottom edges of the ventral scales function like the tread on a tire, gripping the surface and propelling the snake forward. The snake has four modes of propelling itself: concertina, serpentine, sidewinding, and caterpillar (rectilinear). That is why the movement of a snake fascinates the onlooker. Additionally, the snake is crafty, cunning, deceptive, and hypnotizing. Though some snakes may appear to be harmless, they can nevertheless strike with deadly force against innocent bystanders or even their owners. It leaves one wondering why some people have them as pets. The Guardian Newspaper in the UK reported on June 29, 2011 of a man named Luke Yeomans who was killed by one of his pets just days before he was set to open a snake sanctuary in Nottingham. The story reads:

> "A man with a lifelong love of snakes was bitten by one of his king cobras and died, just as he was about to open a breeding colony for the venomous reptiles that grow up to 18 feet long. Luke Yeomans, 47 years of age, was due to open the King Cobra Sanctuary in Nottingham to the public this weekend, but had a heart attack after being bitten. Police said the snake had been contained and there was no danger to the public. Writing on the sanctuary's website previously, Yeomans said it had been born from "my lifelong love for this amazing snake species, and my concerns that it could eventually disappear from the wild".[37]

The man definitely had a natural love for snakes but apparently that snake did not have the same love for him or did not feel like reciprocating his love that day. Unfortunately, it led to his untimely demise. The devil is like that. He is like a deadly snake that seeks to destroy. He has no mercy for his prey no matter how cooperative a person has been to him in the past.

---

[37] Http://www.guardian.co.uk/uk/2011/jun/29/man-dies-bitten-king-cobra. Retrieved December 12, 2011.

When you cease to be useful in his eyes, you are going down. Christians are his prime target. Thank God that the time is coming when he will be completely restrained, but for now, he is the king of this world and is doing everything he can to entrap God's children with the ultimate goal of leading them astray from the truth. The Bible declares in Revelation 12:9 that "The great dragon was hurled down—that ancient serpent called the devil, or Satan, who leads the whole world astray. He was hurled to the earth, and his angels with him." Until this happens, believers need to learn how to deal with the devil, that old snake.

Allow me to suggest a few ways to do so based on Paul's encounter with a snake in Acts 28:1-10. The first thing that is worth mentioning is that the snake came out unexpectedly. It was not Paul's desire to encounter a snake. He did not go looking for it. He did not call it forth. He probably did not know it was there. The devil is like that; he shows up when we least expect him, when we are least prepared, and when we are most vulnerable. That is why the Bible says in Matthew 26:41, "Watch and pray so that you will not fall into temptation. The spirit is willing, but the body is weak."

The second thing we notice is that the snake appeared when a fire was started. When the fire was kindled, no one had in mind that a snake would slide out; the heat forced the snake to show itself. When you start worshipping the Lord and praying, a fire is lit. Your intention may simply be to draw closer to God, or strengthen your spirit man, but the devil is affected. You have stirred up the spiritual atmosphere. You have ignited a spiritual fire and Satan cannot stand the heat. When you start a fire, the devil has to come out. When he comes out, he will either try to threaten you or he will begin to beg you to have mercy on him. The snake came out and tried to threaten Paul. In Luke 8:31, the demons (servants of the 'big snake' Satan) begged Jesus not to command them to go out into the abyss. In both examples, we see that the snake or the demons were at God's mercy. Satan is at your mercy as well. He may try to coerce and terrorize you, but it is all "bluff." He knows the authority that God has given to you. You can either allow yourself to be intimated by him or you can do as Paul and Jesus did. Romans 8:11 says, "And if the Spirit of him who raised Jesus from the dead is living in you, he who raised Christ from the dead will also give life to your mortal bodies through his Spirit, who lives in you."

Thirdly, we notice that the snake attacked the servant of God and no one else. The devil certainly knows who you are and knows that you pose a threat to him. He will therefore try to attack you. The devil knew that wherever Paul went, he preached the Word of God and people got saved; so the devil certainly did not want the entire island of Malta to believe in Christ. The devil did not want the island inhabitants to denounce their allegiance to him and turned their lives over to the control of the Holy Spirit. To prevent this from happening, he had to attack Paul. He may try to do the same thing to you but he is a loser. God has already given you the victory. No demon in hell can stop the plans of God over your life if you do not allow them.

Fourthly, you will notice that the snake did not just bite Paul; it attached itself to his hand. This was probably a Lebentine Viper. This snake does not just bite; it chews on its victim a little bit in order to inject more venom. The snake tries to ensure that its blow will take its victim to the grave. Its poison is deadly! In the same way, the devil wants to fasten himself onto you in any way he can and inflict a lethal blow. You need to declare to the devil that his plans are defeated and that you will live and not die! Premature death shall not be your portion!

Fifthly, Paul shook off the serpent. It was an act of refusal on his part to be attached to it. You have probably noticed that there are few things Paul did not do. He did not scream or shout. He remained calm while others panicked. Also, he did not get angry and accuse the villagers of voodoo or cursing him. Remember that he was the only one who was bitten. Why only him? Paul viewed the situation from a spiritual perspective. He realized that the devil knew his identity and was determined to destroy him, but he knew that it was not God's plan for him to die at that time. While on the storm-tossed ship, an angel had revealed that Paul would live to testify before the Emperor. Therefore, Paul knew for sure that it was not yet his time to die (Romans 27:23-27). Look, do not let the devil plan your life and death. Your life is not his to take. If you belong to Jesus, then it is God's decision and not the devil's. Therefore do not let the devil influence you to panic.

Finally, Paul shook the serpent off into the fire. In other words, he put the serpent right back into the heat where it would be destroyed. Satan knows his destiny. He knows the power that the Lord has given to you. He knows what you are able to do to him in Jesus' name. He knows the power of God that resides in you. The question is, do you know the spiritual authority you possess and are you using those powers for the advancement of the work of God here on the earth? Are you aware of the authority you have in Jesus' name? Are you aware of the fact that your ship is equipped with the most modern, sophisticated technology available in modern history? An eagle knowing what it is made of refuses to allow any bird in the sky to intimidate it. The eagle rules and dominates the sky as king.

From a broader spiritual perspective, this mystery can be interpreted in light of Satan, the serpent, trying to overthrow and destroy the kingdom of Jesus Christ, the rock of our salvation. He tries to "sit" on the church, partake of its glory, blessings, fame and power. Yet, when God opens the eyes His people and the devil sees or hears them approaching with their spiritual artillery, he has no option but to flee. The Bibles admonishes us in James 4:7 to submit ourselves to God, resist the devil and he will flee from us.

The last mystery mentioned in Proverbs 30:18-19 is "the way of an eagle in the sky." This mystery can be naturally explained by the fact that the eagle does not follow a particular track in the sky and it usually takes its own wild course from crag to crag determining its route as it soars upon the winds. But, when one examines in depth how an eagle flies, it becomes clearer that the way of an eagle in the sky is indeed a mystery. It is true that eagles have large and powerful wings, making flight appear effortless. However, a large expenditure of energy is required by the pectoral and supracoracoideus muscles of an eagle to power its huge wings. Though an eagle is strong, capable of sustained flapping flight, it prefers to soar or glide whenever possible, for in gliding the eagle uses less energy and conserves its strength. Consequently, it is only necessary for an eagle to flip its wings less than five minutes during an hour-long flight. To be sure, this is mysterious! He wonders, "How does an eagle know what to do to conserve its energy?" "How does an eagle soar in the sky without any trace?"

As accurate as this natural interpretation may be, "the way of an eagle in the sky" could spiritually represent the mystery of the Christian who has learned to "soar" in Christ. God wants us to come to the realization, understanding, and learning how to "soar in the heavenlies," far above principalities, powers, spiritual wickedness in high places, adversities and the storms of life, relying completely on the power of God. The Father has given this divine nature to us. He wants us to partake of His nature, act like children of the King, and talk like those who have been redeemed by the blood of His only begotten Son, our Lord. When we finally start acting, walking, talking and behaving like "Eagle Christians" we will no longer be content to live with mediocrity. Conversely, we will begin to live as God destined us to live. By the time we arrive at this stage of maturity in our Christian walk, we will cease to do what Solomon describes in Ecclesiastes 10:7: "I have seen slaves on horseback, while princes go on foot like slaves." We will become like an eagle that mounts up and rides on the air currents with hardly any effort. We will begin to live an abundant and victorious Christian life as eagles, not like chickens.

But, the question that is worth addressing is, "How does an eagle get to where it is?" In other words, what can we learn from the life of an eagle, beginning at its birth to when it begins to fly, that can instruct us in our living of the Christian life?

CHAPTER IV

UNDERSTANDING THE EAGLES' PERCEPTION OF MARRIAGE

"The woman was given the two wings of a great eagle,
so that she might fly to the place prepared
for her in the desert,
where she would be taken care of for a time,
times and half a time, out of the serpent's reach"
(Revelation 12:14).

In seeking to understand how eagles manage their "home" or care for their young ones, it might be helpful to take a closer look at the life of an eagle beginning from its conception. In fact, let me begin with the process used by an eagle in selecting a partner for mating and reproduction.

It is not known whether it is the female or the male eagle that initiates the process of choosing a partner. But, what is clear in the mind of each eagle is the fact that the decision of choosing an opposite sex partner is extremely critical, given that it is a once in a lifetime decision. As a result, it must be given serious consideration. Eagles are monogamous and they mate (or in human terms, are married) for life; no amount of trials or challenges will separate them except by death. It is only when one of the pair dies that the other becomes free to look for and take on another partner. Eagles seem to understand God's intent for marriage and they obey it to the letter.

What a beautiful thing to learn as believers! When God created man, He said that it was not good for man to be alone and therefore He made for him a helpmate. God intended marriage to be for life: a lifelong journey! That is why the prophet states in Malachi 2:16 that the Lord hates divorce. It was never His intention for a man and woman to be divorced once they unite in holy matrimony. The Bible declares that it is for this reason a man will leave his father and mother and will unite to his wife, and they will become one flesh.[38] The word, "united" (in some translations it says, cleave), is from the Greek word ενωμένος (enomenos), which conveys the concept of "being glued together". In other words, when a man and a woman unite in holy matrimony, they are "glued together" and are expected to stay together for life.

---

[38] Genesis 2:24

The passage of scripture quoted above is repeated by our Lord Jesus in the gospel of Matthew[39] and underscored by Paul in his letter to the church in Ephesus.[40] I am of the strong conviction that this verse is THE most important verse in the Bible concerning marriage. It gives three principles for marriage that were established by God. I believe that in the eyes of God, for a marriage to be everything that He has designed it to be, these three principles, LEAVING, CLEAVING, and WEAVING must be respected.

"Leaving" has to do with losing your dependency upon your mother, father, or anyone you were relying on before you got married. It certainly does not mean you should abandon your parents or loved ones. It rather has to do with relieving yourself from the emotional, financial, and physical connections that impede your judgment and hinder you from making independent decisions in the interest of your new family. For some people, this is hard, whereas for others, it is not very difficult. Whatever the situation, it is clear that God's intent is for married people to sever the emotional umbilical cord that may still be attached to parents. Some married people have difficulty leaving the parents' home, and even when they do decide to leave, the parents are asked to keep the grown child's room ready just in case the marriage does not work.

---

[39]   Matthew 19:5
[40]   Ephesus 5:31

Sadly, because of the love parents have for their kids, they sometimes reply, "Your room is right here when you need it, don't hesitate for a moment to come back." By so doing, they are not encouraging their kids to leave permanently. It is as if their children are leaving for vacation. Parents apparently expect their child to leave the marriage and return home as their son or daughter again. This is contrary to the teaching of Scripture. We need to remember that when we make the decision to unite in holy matrimony, we are making a life-long decision to leave parents and be joined to a spouse, and there will be no turning back. That is exactly what eagles do. They leave and they cleave. In fact, eagles leave before they even find a mate. They venture out into the world and live on their own. They endure tough times and understand the times. They hunt for themselves independent of their parents. They fight fierce battles and mount the winds. They master the art of "no retreat, no surrender." They know that their parents have moved on to build a new family of eaglets, and even if they wanted to return, it would be impossible.

I do not intend to sound insensitive but this is God's plan: a man will LEAVE his father and mother and unite to his wife. As a matter of fact, you will never find an eagle parent approaching a group of eagles in order to solicit a mate for a young adult eagle. Father eagle or mother eagle has nothing to do with their young adult eagle choosing a partner for life. The training process begins as soon as an eagle is born. Eagles do not wait until their children are grown and ready to choose a mate before they start training them on how to be a good partner, father or mother. My admonishment to fathers—teach your boys to soar as eagles from the day they are brought into this world. Speak into your sons' lives and bless them materially, spiritually, emotionally, psychologically, and culturally, before they embark on that journey of no return. Do what is needed before it is too late. When they make the decision to fly away, bid them farewell. Pray for them but do not encourage them to come back. Let them go! Do not work long hours while your children are young and then try to make up for the lost time of their training when you are old and they should already be off on their own. It just might be too late. Mothers, do the same with your daughters, please. Release your girls and let them leave when it is time. The best thing that you can do for them is to continually commit them into the hands of the Lord. God prepared, supported, encouraged, kept, protected, and guided you. Why would He not do the same for your children? Place them in the hands of the Lord as they leave your hands.

Let me quickly point out also that the concept of letting go applies not only to parents and grown children, but to anyone or anything that has the potential to disrupt or interfere with your marriage. You must be willing to let that person or thing go. Even if it is a close and dear friend who has walked with you through thick and thin and you know that he or she will interfere in your relationship with your spouse, you must be willing to break the relationship or take concrete steps to ensure that he or she does not interfere with your marriage. You just cannot afford to have anyone or anything influence your independent judgment when dealing with your spouse and kids. You must LEAVE them in order to fulfill God's purpose for your life.

The next stage in the process after Leaving is Cleaving. This is God's second principle for marriage.

As previously mentioned, the word "cleave" has to do with being glued together or bonded to something. It is the same word that describes how leprosy clings to the body (II Kings 5:27). In his agony, Job explained how bones cling to the skin and cannot be separated (Job 19:20). That is exactly what happens in marriage: two becoming one. Anyone can certainly argue that it is easier said than done and that argument would be valid. For a couple that is dating and deeply in love, it is easy for them to accept that the two of them shall become one but after they get married, they start to wonder and argue which one of them they would like to become.

When you exchange marriage vows, it is intended for life. It is a vow you make to God, to your partner, to yourself, your parents, relatives and loved ones. This vow is made before the invisible cloud of witnesses, angels, and those yet to be born. Therefore, it should be a vow of permanence. That is why the Lord declares in Malachi 2:13-16 that a man ought to remember the wife of his youth. This is an admonition for you not to change your attitude towards your spouse just because he or she is looking older or has put on a few more pounds. Do not change your marriage commitment now because your spouse has worked hard over the years and has a few wrinkles on his or her face. Do not change now because she cannot bear any more children for you. Do not change now because he or she cannot do everything that was done for you in the past. Do not change now because you have seen someone else who appears to be more youthful, and beautiful or handsome. REMEMBER your commitment! Never say, "She was not like this when I married her . . . . He was never like that!" REMEMBER AND CLEAVE!

In first Peter 3:7, the Apostle writes, "Husbands, in the same way be considerate as you live with your wives, and treat them with respect as the weaker partner and as heirs with you of the gracious gift of life, so that nothing will hinder your prayers." We cannot change the fact that before marriage (in most instances), opposites attract; after marriage, opposites have the tendency to irritate or repel. Always remember what attracted you to your spouse in the first place and then Cleave.

You have probably read or heard the story of a study conducted with both male and female scientists. They were asked if a computer should be called he or she. As the story goes, the women scientists said it should be called "he" because of the following reasons: a) In order to get their attention, you have to turn them on; b) they are supposed to solve problems, but half the time they are the problem; c) as soon as you commit to one, you realize that if you had waited a little longer, you would have gotten a better model. The men scientists strongly disagreed and suggested that a computer should be referred to as "she" because: a) no one can understand the internal logic of a computer except its creator; b) even the smallest mistakes are stored in long-term memory; c) as soon as you commit to one, you find yourself spending half your paycheck on accessories for it. These statements, I believe are humorous but they have a certain measure of truth to them. If we are not mindful, we will be trying to get out of our marriage as quickly as we jumped into it. If we are looking for problems, we will find them, but if we are looking for solutions, many are available. In other words, if you want to find reasons for which you should stop cleaving to your spouse, you will have no difficulty finding many.

This reminds me of a story about a pastor who was pondering how he could raise money at church. After a while, he ran out of strategies until one Sunday, while driving to Church, he had this epiphany. Overjoyed at the revelation he had received, he carefully planned how the fundraising would be done. He would ask the men in the church to give generously based on the beauty of their wives. Being confident of the fact that no man would give less than a hundred dollars, especially given the fact that their wives will be sitting next to them, he congratulated himself on his creativity. When the service began, he announced the fund-raising project. Almost all the men gave huge amounts just as he anticipated. Near the end of the fundraising, a man stood, walked to the altar and placed a dollar in the basket. Astonished, the pastor, called out to him, "Brother, this must be a mistake. You placed a dollar in the basket. Your wife is certainly more beautiful than the value of a dollar." The man turned around and replied, "Pastor, you certainly don't know my wife. If you saw her, you'd give me back some change." Ouch! If this was actually a true story and this man's wife was present, imagine the embarrassment and humiliation she must have felt. Quite frankly, I do not think this actually happened. If it did, then all I can say is "What a pity!"

In order to be theologically accurate, it must be stated that the word "cleave" is the same Hebrew word "*dabaq*" which appears 53 times in the Old Testament.[41] It is the exact word that is used to describe Ruth's action towards her mother-in-law after the death of her husband. She made a conscious decision not to leave even when Orpah kissed Naomi farewell and Naomi insisted that she (Ruth) should return to her people. Ruth refused to be moved by the situation and though she had every reason to return to her own people and reestablish herself; she decided to "cleave" or to remain "united" to Naomi. Her decision was not based on economic prosperity or the prospect of remarriage. On the contrary, it was against logic, cultural norms and common sense. Naomi was old and could not bear sons again, and even if she did, they would be too young for Ruth to marry one of them. Additionally, Naomi was poor and did not have the finances to take care of herself and Ruth. In spite of all that, Ruth decided to "cleave." Some translations say: Ruth would not be parted from her (BBE); Ruth held on to her (CEV); Ruth insisted on staying with Naomi (NLT); Ruth held on to her tightly (NET).[42]

---

[41] Ruth Commentary 1:14-18. http://www.preceptaustin. org/ruth_114-22.htm. Retrieved January 16, 2012

[42] In order to fully understand why Ruth decided to cleave to Naomi and how the Lord blessed her, read chapter IV of my book entitled, *Turning Your Mess Into A Message*, AuthorHouse, 2011.

In Deuteronomy 10:20, we are told to "Fear the LORD our God and serve Him. **Hold fast** to Him and take your oaths in His name." In the same book, Moses instructs us to love the Lord our God, walk in His ways and **hold fast** to Him" (11:22). Holding fast to God is the same as cleaving to Him. It is spiritual, but also has intellectual, emotional, physical, financial, cultural and moral implications. It conveys the idea of wholehearted commitment of one's spirit, soul and body to God but also to one's spouse. It is this concept that eagles understand so well that when an eagle selects a life-long partner, nothing but death separates them. In the same way, when we select a life partner, we ought to clearly see the challenges of being married to that person, understand them, and yet decide to continue on in faith and hope. Somehow, we ought to believe that this is the best deal God has for us or else, we should not get married in the first place. We must honestly desire to live with spouses the way they are or pray that the Holy Spirit will make the needed changes in their lives. A popular prayer for many situations, including marriage, is one by *Reinhold Niebuhr,* known as the Serenity Prayer. The first part of the prayer states, "God grant me the serenity to accept the things I cannot change; courage to change the things I can; and the wisdom to know the difference." This is the attitude that the Lord expects us to have. There will be things you will be able to change in your marriage, but I can assure you that there will be many others you will not be able to change. For the latter, you need to pray honestly that the Lord will grant you the serenity to accept them with the right attitude.

The final principle for marriage given by the Lord is WEAVING. It has to do with "becoming one flesh." To word "weave" means to interlace thread, yarns, strips, or other fibers to create a new fabric or material. It also means to form by combining various elements or details into a connected whole.[43] Weaving, whether interlacing threads or combining human elements to form a connected whole, is a process. It is a tedious job that takes time, requires patience, and demands artistry. For some people, weaving fabric is their profession; they invest hours and weave fabrics. Marriage is also a process of investment that is carried out over a lifetime. It does not just happen; is not instantaneous simply because one wishes it to happen or because a "few magic words" are said: "I therefore pronounce you as husband and wife."

What is interesting about the weaving process is that a good weave usually involves three strands. When you examine a braid, it may appear as if only two strands of hair were twisted together, but in reality

---

[43] Weave. Dictionary.com. *Dictionary.com Unabridged*. Random House, Inc. http://dictionary.reference.com/browse/weave (accessed: January 23, 2012).

there is always a third, not immediately evident, but it plays a significant role in keeping the other two closely woven. Were you to pull the third strand, the other two would become weakened and eventually fall apart. Apparently that is what the wise, ancient author of Ecclesiastes meant when he states in Ecclesiastes 4:12, "Though one may be overpowered, two can defend themselves. A cord of three strands is not quickly broken." He clearly states the values of having two in comparison to one; but then he goes on to say, "A cord of three (not two) is not quickly broken." The two individuals being "glued together" are becoming one flesh, but the third person intertwined in this relationship is God, for it is His institution. Therefore, He is intimately involved. He is that third strand, not immediately evident, but present today; and who has already promised to be with you, and all of us, to the very end of the age.

It must be noted that the Lord does not impose Himself as the third strand. He is a gentleman and must be invited into the relationship before He can come in and take His rightful place.

Couples need to understand and accept unconditionally that weaving is a lifelong process and starts with sharing everything in common. Eagles become one in the sense that they share everything in common. They look out for each other, serve each other, communicate with each other, encourage each other and grow together. They basically have no hidden secret or agenda.

I remember counseling couples and the wife said, "My cell phone is mine and he has no right to look in it." Then the husband said, "If that is the case, then my money is mine and your money is yours. We will not have a joint account. I will pay my share of the bills and you will pay yours." I became sad and said, "The both of you are not living out God's intent for your marriage. You are simply acting as roommates or housemates."

I know that in some instances you need to be mindful when beginning a new relationship because of the many "wolves" that come in sheep's clothing (Matthew 7:15), but that should be an exception to the rule and you should have valid reasons for wanting to separate those essential things that build trust, understanding, and confidence in the marriage. You need to understand that weaving involves or demands combined efforts; working as a team. It also requires time, energy and money. You have to make the time needed to be with your partner. That is what eagles do. They spend time together, work together and make room for each other's mistakes. I am not one hundred percent sure how they do it, but I believe that eagles do forgive each other. It is very rare to see a male and a female eagle (couple) fighting. It is likely that one in the eagle couple would accidentally bump into the other while flying or in some other way disappoint or offend the other eagle, but they do not leave or abandon the union because of the offense. They seem to have a way of forgiving each other and moving on. They realize, as in the game of football, you do not tackle the player wearing the same color uniform you have, or you would be hindering the progress of your own team. Fighting your spouse is not the solution. You should both present a united front and fight together against the devil and his demonic forces.

Obviously, I am not trying to imply that everything will be easy or that a marriage vow must NEVER be broken. To think or imply that would be very naïve on my part. The reality is that we do live in a broken world and we are fallen creatures living by God's grace. Nevertheless, in spite of our sinful state, God still wants His children to take marriage very seriously. Jesus said, "What therefore God has joined together, let no man separate (Mark 10:9). Also, read I Corinthians 7:10-11 and Hebrews 13:4 and you will see God's heart for marriage. Having said that, I need to point out that the Holy Scripture is sensitive to the challenges we face, but for many of us we do not want to face problems in this life and therefore divorce has become the easy way out. Jesus said to His disciples before His departure to heaven, "I have told you these things, so that in me you may have peace. In this world you will have trouble. But take heart! I have overcome the world" (John 16:33). When faced with challenges in our marriage then, we forget God's principles for marriage. We ignore the fact that He wants us to leave, cleave and weave. We forget the fact that it is a process that takes many years; perhaps up to the day we enter the grave. We forget that God is not finished working on us. We forget that we also had a part to play in the dysfunction of our marriage, and the challenges that confront us in the marriage were not caused only by our partner. We forget how many times others have forgiven us of our shortcomings and yet we are quick to hold onto and refuse to forgive the mistakes of our partner. Yes, we do forget so easily, don't we?

Some may argue, and rightfully so, that the problem is that we have inadvertently adapted behaviors from our surrounding culture which have negative consequences on our marriage. One classic example is the fact that we live in a "microwave" and "fast food" society. This has influenced us to have low tolerance and we easily become impatient with one another. We want things to happen quickly and if they do not, we move on because we have many choices and options. We therefore see no need to put up with or help someone who is lazy, inefficient and ineffective, lacks understanding, or slow in bringing the world down at our feet. We want everything to be quick, easy and instantly available. When we want an answer, we expect it to come this instant. When we have a headache, we want instant relief. When we want food, we go to a fast food restaurant because we want it this instant. When we want political solutions from Washington and do not get them instantly, we vote our leaders out of office. Similarly, when we have a problem at home and our partner cannot instantly solve it or help us solve it, we kick him or her out and find someone else. We are not willing to be patient one with another, fight for what we value, nurture and groom what we desire and give God the time to complete what He started. We are like the guy who prayed, "Lord I know that I need patience. I really do. Can you please give it to me? And by the way, can you do it right now?"

For others, the issue is not impatience, but the unwillingness to forgive and let go of the past. We easily forget the teaching of scripture in 1 Corinthians 13 regarding love. We forget that if we say we have committed ourselves and our love to someone, then we must also remember that love is patient, kind, does not envy, does not boast and is not proud. Love does not dishonor others, is not self-seeking, is not easily angered and it keeps no records of wrongs. Love does not delight in evil but rejoices with the truth. Additionally, love always protects, always trusts, always hopes, and always perseveres. Most importantly, LOVE NEVER FAILS!

Please hear my pastor's heart as I write this: I am not condemning those who have gone through divorce or are currently going through divorce. However, I do not wish to encourage those who see divorce as an easy way out of a difficult marriage. Divorce is unscriptural and ungodly. You may think that the grass is greener on the other side but you might be disappointed when you get there and find out it is not as green as you thought it was. I know beyond the shadow of doubt that some people are experiencing hell in their marriages.

I am deeply saddened and heartbroken when I hear some of the things people do to those they have vowed to love and cherish in this life. Consequently, when a couple is going through the process of divorce, though it is not the best option, it is quite common to hear those who know of their struggles say, "We understand, we empathize with you, we feel your pain," or simply, "We are not sure what we would do if we were in your situation." Sometimes, all we can do in such a situation is offer support to and prayers on that person's behalf.

How I wish that the only reasons people sought divorce were due to adultery, abuse, or abandonment, but you and I both know that many times the pursuit of divorce is, quite frankly, self-centered, ungodly, cruel, disrespectful, evil, and a gross disregard for God's Word. You might be thinking that I am passing judgment on others. I have had people say to me, "I know God is forgiving, and therefore I know He will forgive me for the sin of divorce as well." To them the Apostle Paul addressed these words, "What shall we say then? Shall we go on sinning so that grace may increase?[44] The Apostle is quick to give the answer to his rhetorical question by stating the obvious: "By no means! We died to sin; how can we live in it any longer?"[45] The undeniable verity is that the Bible condemns divorce and so must we as God's children. It does not matter if the person is dear to me and I long to be merciful to them. It does not change the fact that God hates divorce. I could give all the justifications or excuses found in any book, but the truth remains that God hates divorce. Yahweh is a covenant-keeping God and since marriage is a picture of Christ and the Church, we are to be covenant-keepers, as well. People who disregard the covenant of marriage do not understand the depth, strength and beauty of God's covenant. We do much, daily, to cause Him to "divorce" us, but because of His covenant with the Church through Christ, He keeps wooing His Bride back into fellowship with Him instead of "divorcing"

---

[44] Romans 6:1
[45] Romans 6:2

us. Praise to our merciful and gracious God! If this biblical explanation does not suffice, then when we get to heaven, we will certainly ask God for a better explanation. Until that glorious opportunity is granted to us, we have to live with the fact that God hates divorce and if we want to be pleasing in His sight, we must remain married except for the conditions stated in the Bible.[46]

The point that I am trying to make is that for many marriages that end up in divorce, the fundamental reasons for pursuing divorce in the first place are not usually related to adultery (extramarital affair), abuse (physical, emotional, and psychological), or abandonment (desertion of the home and family). Some claim, "I don't love her anymore." Others say, "I am no longer happy in this marriage and I know that God wants me to be happy." To these people, I think Dr. Gary Smalley would say, "Love is a Decision."[47]

---

[46] The Bible seems to only give two reasons for divorce. The first is adultery. See Matthew 19:9. The Greek for immorality is *porneia* from which we get the word pornography, and sexual immorality. Hence, adultery, it appears, is a ground for divorce according to Jesus. The second is abandonment. Paul wrote in 1 Corinthians 7:15, "Yet if the unbelieving one leaves, let him leave; the brother or the sister is not under bondage in such cases, but God has called us to peace."

[47] Dr Gary Smalley with John Trent wrote a book entitled: *Love is a Decision, proven techniques to keep your marriage alive and lively*. Thomas Nelson, 2001. This book

You made the decision to get married and it is time to make the decision to stay married. It is true that it takes two to make the marriage work, but are you doing what is required of you to make it work? Do you have the mindset of "No matter what, I want my marriage back; I am willing to make it work?" Have you said to yourself and truly believe in your heart that you are ready to make the necessary sacrifices in order for peace, love and happiness to be restored to the relationship? Or, have you entrenched yourself in the position, "If she changes first, then I will too"?

Christians, like unbelievers, are unfortunately becoming increasingly uncommitted to the marital vows made in the presence of God, our partner, and the witnesses present during our marriage ceremony. This lack of commitment makes Christians vulnerable to ridicule in the eyes of the world since the divorce rate in the church is the same as it is in world. We have failed to protect the sanctity of marriage. On the one hand, Christian men have failed to love their wives as Christ loved the church and gave Himself for it, while on the other hand, wives have failed to submit to their own husbands as their head of their homes.

------

is a good book on marriage and I do highly recommend it for couples who are struggling in their marriage or who need to reenergize (spice up) their marriage.

I believe that couples sometimes enter into what ought to be lifetime commitment not fully understanding the permanence of their vows or with a faulty mindset that they can walk out of the marriage anytime they choose. I heard a story of a pastor who was conducting a wedding and he asked the bride, "Do you promise to love . . . . here present, in good times and bad times; in sickness and in health; in riches and in poverty, so help you God?" She replied, "Yes, no, no, yes, yes, no." Confused by her answer, the pastor asked, "What do you mean?" She answered, "I promise to love him in good times but I do not think that I will be able to handle it when things go bad. I know that I will love him when he is healthy, but I do not do well around sick people. I also definitely know that I will shower him with love given all the riches he has, but he better not to go bankrupt. I do not want to suffer. I have had my fair share of suffering in this life and by marrying him, I am kissing suffering good bye." Does this sound familiar? Some of us may be appalled at this woman's comment while others might say, "At least she's being honest about how she feels." And speaking of honesty, isn't she expressing the very thing many people think but do not actually verbalize on their wedding day?

In contrast, eagles are monogamous, mating for life. Whatever the storm or calamities that befall them, they remain faithful. They do not go around looking for every Dick, Tom or Harry to replace Jim, John and Jones.

I once heard it said that there are three stages in marriage: The first stage is the ideal. The second stage is the ordeal. And the third stage is the new deal. The first (ideal) stage is what I like to refer to as the fantasy stage. During this stage, those not yet married fantasize about what marriage will be: the physical characteristics of the mate; height, age; looks; mannerisms, intelligence, strength, muscle tone, education, and so forth. This is the "dreaming stage." Love birds dream of how wonderful it will be. This stage can also be called the "sleeping beauty" stage when the girl dreams of Prince charming coming to rescue her and giving her that kiss that will wake her up and they will live happily ever after.

Eagles do not fantasize. They face reality. They know that marriage is for life and there is more to marriage than dreams, money or good looks. They know that marriage requires commitment or a "stick-to-itiveness." It is only for adults and kids need not apply. I use the word "adult" not referring to chronological age but in reference to maturity, stability, understanding, determination, and a strong sense of purpose in life. Some people may have the years, but they are kids at heart and need to grow up before they get into trouble. They may look strong, grown up, muscular, but they are still kids within. They are still playing with toys. They are still running to mommy to cook their favorite soup even when they get married. They are still running to daddy, incapable of making decisions that vitally affect their home.

During the ideal stage, we fantasize about how our marriage will be. Unfortunately, after marriage, our dreams are replaced with reality and the stark difference stops us from looking ahead in hope for the good that could yet be. Our eyesight becomes limited to the "here and now," seeing only in the natural and finding fault with it. For some, just a few days after getting married, they realize that it is not quite what they thought it would be. This leads to the desire to want to get out of the marriage. Beloved, we as believers need to accept the fact that marriage will never be perfect simply because we are not perfect. You are an imperfect being and so is your spouse. Even Adam and Eve's marriage was not perfect because they sinned. Even the best of marriages know times of breakdown, doubt, disillusionment, anger, distress and conflict. Conflict in marriage is inevitable. In the final analysis, what matters is how we deal with the daily conflicts we encounter. Having conflict is not an indication that the union cannot or will not work. We therefore need to learn to focus on our assets (strengths) and not on our liabilities (weaknesses). The other thing that may be helpful in dealing with conflict in marriage is your own attitude. If you have the right attitude and seek to develop the needed skills in conflict resolution, you will be able to remain married by the grace of God.

The second stage in marriage, the ordeal stage, is when the couple is finished romanticizing and reality sets in. They begin to see each other without "make up" and realize that the other person snores, makes scary noises at night while sleeping, has some unrevealed secrets, and most disappointingly, he or she is not as "cool" as previously supposed. With awakened realization, you fear you have turned your freedom over to a "total stranger" who is ready to take you for a ride, use you as a slave, empty your bank account, or make you feel like an idiot in spite of all that you try to do to please him or her. You begin to ask yourself, "What did I get myself into? What was I thinking? Why did I not listen to my mommy or friends? How can I get out?" The situation is further compounded when you realize that you have gone a little too deep; either you are pregnant or have gotten so deep in debt that you will not be able to handle the bills all by yourself. Additionally, you may start to wonder, "What will others say about me?"

The "ordeal stage" is very dangerous. It can lead to a state of frustration, unhappiness, depression, unfaithfulness, and sadly, suicide. It is at this point that you need the help of God Almighty. It is at this point that you need the community of believers. It is at this point you need your faith in God. It is at this point you need to seek advice from the Word of God. It is at this point that you need the Lord to send His ministering angels to come and tend to your spirit man and do warfare on your behalf. At this point, you cannot afford to remain in this state for long. You must break out of it before it destroys you. Pray and set yourself free. Speak the promises of God over your life. Seek counseling if necessary. Do not just sit and expect it to pass. You must consciously decide to move on to the final and most critical stage as quickly as possible. That stage is the "New Deal."

This final stage determines if you will remain married or if you will seek divorce. It also determines the quality of your marriage. At this stage, you have three choices:

1) **Settle**: You can take on a nonchalant attitude or what I like to call the "blah, blah, blah." It is like entering a hot or cold tub of water. At first the temperature seems uncomfortable and you immediately want to leave, but as you stay, your body gets used to the temperature and you decide not to leave. At the "new deal" stage, you decide to stay in the marriage because of the kids, the social pressure of your church and family, or to maintain your social status. Consequently, you and your spouse start living like

roommates and you begin to pour your life into other things. When the opportunity does present itself, you strike at him or her through occasional verbal attacks, put-downs and other unkind behaviors.

2) **Bail out**: The second option is to bail out of your marriage. The average length of marriages in America is approximately 8 years. Sadly, many marriages do not survive the first few months. Bail out appears to be the easier option for many folks. They assert, "I don't have the time and energy for this . . . . I am out of here."

3) **Build**: You can decide to build your marriage or fight to make it work. When the decision is made that you want to keep your marriage in spite of all the challenges found therein then, you enter the last stage, which is the "New Deal."

The "New Deal" stage is where you decide to seek for a change in your marriage. You realize that God will be your helper. You realize that you will not get everything the exact way you dreamed and therefore you will need to compromise. You realize you are partly responsible for the existing challenges and you agree to seek change within yourself, trusting that the Lord will work on your partner. You realize that things may not be as bad as they seem. You come to rely on God to make the necessary changes in both of your lives for the betterment of the marriage. It is at this point God, the third strand in the marriage, begins to work.

Perhaps one reason we have so many problems in marriages today is because we do not take the time to thoughtfully scrutinize the one to whom we are committing ourselves for life. Some people make hasty decisions to marry, especially when they envision an associated element of "glamour." As believers, some of us do not take the time to ask God for His leading and direction. You see, a female eagle is usually not in a hurry to get married. She is self-assured of her own abilities and identity and feels no rush to pick up just any male eagle that comes along to be her mate for life. The female eagle is the one who makes the final decision of whether she will accept a male as her lifelong partner. She will not mate with him or any other male eagle until she makes that decision. The female eagle seems to have her standards set in her mind. She knows what she wants and knows if those qualities can be found in a male eagle that is expressing interest in her. A few ornithologists (those who study birds) believe that color might be a factor since the male and female eagle pairs generally look alike. Some ornithologists believe the size of the eagle is also a determining factor, given the fact that within the pair, the female is always larger than the male.

Eagles are also known to conduct "courtship flights" or "sky dancing" before they become husband and wife. These aerial acrobatics involve locking talons and tumbling down, without flight, through the sky together. This entails risk-taking and is a clear demonstration of the highest level of commitment and a strong desire to want to be with that partner even if it would lead to one or both of the eagles losing their lives.

You will find it fascinating to know as well that the female eagle, before choosing her partner for life, takes a male eagle through a series of tests I refer to as "ordeals" or "life defining moments" intended to test his resolve, strength, dexterity, motion, commitment and courage. This test involves the use of twigs. At first, the female takes a twig and flies into a tree. She then releases the twig, expecting the male who is dating her to catch it before it hits the ground. If he succeeds, she finds a larger twig, comparable in size and weight to an eaglet. This time, she flies a little higher up the tree and releases the twig, still expecting her "admirer" to catch it before it touches the ground. If he is not successful, the courtship is literally over and she moves on with her life. However, if he passes the test, he moves to the last and final feat. This time, the female eagle (also known as the hen-eagle) searches for and finds a branch weighing as much as she does, and then she flies high up into the tallest tree she can find. Upon reaching the pinnacle, she drops the branch, expecting the male eagle (also called a tierce) to catch it before it touches the ground. If he succeeds, he has passed the test and she will allow him to mate with her, consummating their union. If he fails, the test is over and she will have nothing more to do with him. Recall that the female is usually bigger than the male eagle, therefore for him to try to mate with her against her will would be pointless and obviously dangerous.

By now you may be wondering why the female eagle takes the male through such ordeals before she will commit herself to a life-long relationship. For me, the reasons are simple. The first test is intended to give him an opportunity to demonstrate his level of commitment to her and their unborn children. She wants proof that he knows how to overcome minor, yet dangerous obstacles in life. You see, the first twig is small and light. When released from a distance above the ground, the twig could be blown about by the wind. Additionally, the fact that it is not too far above the ground, the male eagle could be hit by a car, run into another tree, or a pole while trying to catch it. In the mind of the female eagle, if the male eagle is unwilling to sacrifice his life now for her and the relationship, what proof does she have that he would be willing to do so in the future?

The second test is intended to see if he would care enough to abandon whatever he is doing and quickly come to the rescue of his own eaglet if it were ever in imminent danger. Additionally, the male eagle must demonstrate that if he ever needed to rescue a falling eaglet, he has the strength to do so and to restore it to safety.

Finally, the last test is an opportunity for the male eagle to prove that he is not only able to and willing to fight for his family by using his instinctive and acquired skills as a male eagle, but to show to his wife-to-be that he is not going to abandon her and her kids when the storms of life start raging or when he is faced with a challenge that may involve him laying down his life to save his family. Remember that the female eagle is usually bigger than the male and the final branch that the female chooses is usually her size. That means that the branch chosen by the female may be bigger and heavier than the male eagle. The female eagle needs to be convinced that her future mate will be willing to stand up to their enemies in spite of his size and fight to the end, rescuing her and taking her to safety if she needs his help.

Are you a female who is already married? Did you subject your spouse to a series of tests? Did he pass the tests or did you just marry him because you wanted to get married? If you are single, please do not rush into marriage. Reread this chapter and allow the Lord to guide your step. Set your standards (be reasonable) and pray. Do not give yourself to any man or woman just because of sweet-talking or good looks. Words can be "empty" and looks can be deceptive. Have faith in the Lord that He will bring the right person at the right time. You are very precious to Him and He wants the best for you. If it is seems to be taking a long time, remember you do not want to have that person until God is finished with His work of preparation. Be patient, God will bring him/her. May God's best be your portion!

Chapter V

Understanding How Eagles
Raise Their Family

"Like an eagle that stirs up its nest and hovers over its young,
that spreads its wings to catch them and carries them aloft.
The Lord alone led him; no foreign god was with him"
(Deuteronomy 32:11-12).

In some societies, certain roles have been relegated to women and others to men. For example, in some societies husbands expect the preparation of the meal, cleaning of the house, taking care of the kids (bathing, changing diapers, and reading bedtime stories) to be the responsibility of the wives. In additional to those household tasks, women are expected, for the most part, to work outside of the home in order to contribute to the financial upkeep of the home. Many men who work eight hours a day spend the rest of their day after work, relaxing before the television set, visiting with friends and family members, or simply doing other things that have little or nothing to do with their household or raising their kids. Taking a child to a doctor's appointment, game, musical rehearsal, and so forth are assumed to be part of the mother's job description. Yet, interestingly, when the child turns out be "successful", we as men attempt to take all the credit for something we did not do. Conversely, when the child falls short of dad's expectation, the mother is automatically blamed. It is at this time when you hear comments from dads, "Go talk to your child" or, "Your child doesn't know how to behave or respect others." At that point, we as father completely forget the fact that we neglected our child's upbringing by not investing quality time and properly serving in the role of a father.

All around the world, with America being no exception, there exists moral failure in our societies primarily because fathers are either physically spiritually, emotionally, or psychologically absent in the lives of their children. This is a problem that has existed for generations and appears to be getting worse each day. It needs to be corrected immediately. The involvement of men in the lives of their children is on a downward spiral and if not seen and addressed as an infectious plague that is threatening to further deteriorate the moral fabric of society, we might one day awake to find this world in chaos. It might bring about the judgment of God upon the earth as in the days of old when it was said, "In those days there was no king in Israel; every man did what was right in his own eyes" (Judges 17:6; 21:25). This epidemic exists because, for the most part, men are engulfed in a materialistic culture. They constantly buy things they do not need, with money they do not have, to impress people they do not like. The result is unaffordable and unjustified debts. Unfortunately, when faced with huge debt after unwise and unnecessary spending, the man is left with two options: a) find additional employment to bring in more money (resulting in even less family time); or b) distance himself from the family or become such a "pain" in the home that divorce becomes the only option in order for the rest of the family members to have peace of mind. Either way, the result is that the family becomes fatherless.

God spoke sadly to the Prophet Ezekiel in Ezekiel 22:30, "I sought for a man among them that should make up the hedge, and stand in the gap before me for the land, that I should not destroy it: but I found none." Where are the men who should stand in the gap? Where are the men who should be priests in their homes? Where are the men who are living righteous lives and whose lives inhibit the Lord from destroying the land? Where are the men who should be walking their daughters to the altar and giving those young men the look that says, "You better not mess with my little princess or you will have to answer to me!"

Where are the men that should be role models for the young boys? Are you a man? Is the Lord still looking or has He stopped since He found you? Can He count on you?

Let me take my line of questioning a bit further and ask a more confrontational question: where are the older black men? Who will mentor the younger black men who are in desperate need of father figures? Who will tell them how to be productive citizens and stay out of jail? Where are the older black men who will dress properly and show young black boys, through modeling, how to dress properly so they'll stop walking in public with their pants falling off their behinds thinking it is "cool"? Where are these men?

What we, as humans (especially fathers) fail to do within our families, eagles carry out in theirs with utmost diligence. Eagles understand that the raising of eaglets is both the male's and female's responsibilities. They realize that if their young ones are to be successful in life, both the father and mother have to be involved in the process. They understand that God has given each of them unique roles to play in the lives of their young ones. They know that just as it takes two to conceive, it also takes two to care for the baby. That is why from conception, the male eagle does not run off to find another female to impregnate or he does not suddenly get busy with work, hunting down and killing other creatures. On the contrary, he stays and helps his spouse deal with the complexities associated with giving birth (laying eggs). In fact, before they begin to have babies, the male eagle helps in getting a place ready for the laying of the eggs. He helps in building a comfortable and secure nest. In fact, he does not just build a nest anywhere. He takes into consideration the environment. He tries to find out if the area is infested with dangerous snakes or other predators that would pose significant threats to the young ones. If it is, he does not build the nest there. Additionally, if he is building the nest in the trees, he examines and tests the branch of the tree on which he is expecting to build the nest. His primary concern becomes whether the branch is strong enough to withstand a storm. Obviously, he would not want the branch to collapse or break after the eggs are laid or when there is a storm or strong wind.

After looking for, finding, and determining that the area is conducive for raising his family, the couple starts to gather the materials they need to build their nest. Interestingly, they do not wait until it is time to lay the eggs before they start looking. They prepare for the arrival of the young ones in advance. Both the male and female eagles realize that there is no abortion clinic and no female right-to—lay-the-egg advocates or legislation. Hence, once conception takes place, the eggs must be laid. I think they also realize that their eaglets have the right to life, and God, the Creator of this universe, gave that right to them.

When the female lays the eggs, the male's job does not end at that point. In fact, one can even argue that is when his job actually begins. One of the many things he does from this point is to share the responsibility with the female of sitting on the eggs. Both parents therefore sit on the eggs. This is called incubation and its intent is to keep the eggs warm and protected. The warmth from the parent bird makes sure that the eaglets inside develop properly. Here is something else that I found quite interesting as I studied about the incubation process. I found out that as the parents sit on the eggs in order to keep them warm, a special warm patch grows on their tummies. Some of their feathers drop out so that the warm skin touches the eggs. This is called the brood patch. In other words, the male goes around from this point with a bald tummy. There is no way to hide that he is married and is having babies. It is an indication to the world that he is expecting a child or children. He cannot lie about it or try to cover up with a nice suit. He does not have that luxury. He is a part of the process of helping his kids develop from the moment they are conceived. Additionally, when the father is not sitting on the eggs, he is out patrolling for intruders that might pose a threat to mom and the eggs. When he spots an intruder who is trying to enter his territory, he does everything he can to drive it away. It is worth mentioning also that the eggs are never left alone for a long period of time. One of the parents is always around.

When the eggs hatch and the little ones come forth, both the male and female eagles feed, clean and protect the young ones. When one goes to find food, the other stays in the nest to protect and care for the young ones. To the eagles, raising a family is a responsibility that belongs to both parents. God has given us this same task but unfortunately, some of us see it and act differently. We know what our responsibilities are and what God expects from us, but in most instances, we turn our back and look the other way, especially fathers.

I am who I am today simply because of the grace of God. Like some of you reading this book, I did not have the joy of growing up in a home with both of my parents present. My mom and dad actually separated when I was only three months old, though they remained legally married, until my dad died in 2009. I never got to see or really know my mother until I was thirteen years old. My dad was constantly gone from home. Therefore at a very young age, he turned me over to his mother (my grandmother) who was blind. She reared me until I was thirteen and then my mother's boyfriend found out about me and came to get me from my grandmother. He and my mom took me in and my life became a living hell. There was no social worker to report child abuse and the school authority did not even care or did not have the power to do anything about a child who was being abused or neglected. God had to intervene. He had to rescue me from destruction. There were days that I sat and cried endlessly not knowing if life was worth living. I was constantly told that I was an unwanted child in the home. I was reminded daily that I was as unwanted as an infested, oozing sore on a foot; my very presence was an annoying nuisance. Whenever an opportunity presented itself, and there were plenty of them, I was reminded that I did not belong in that household. I could not enter my parents' (mother and stepfather's) room because it was off limits for me, yet my half siblings could enter, play with them on their bed and receive the affection I craved. Maybe that is why I appreciate God so much. During those times, I found consolation in Him as my Shepherd. There were times when I knew that someone was looking out for me and that person cared deeply. I knew that I was not alone and that it was going to be okay in the end. Is that your story as well? By your action or lack thereof, are you making this your child's story?

When the eagle eggs hatch, the eaglets open their eyes expecting something from their daddy and mommy. Primarily, they expect to be fed. Eaglets have a seemingly insatiable desire for food. Eaglets know that when they open their mouths, Dad and Mom are going to fill them with good things. Therefore, they constantly expect and request food and their expectations are never cut short. Their parents do everything they can to provide their daily needs. That is what God does for us and that is what He expects us to do for our children.

In Psalms 81:10, we read, "I am the Lord thy God which brought you out of the land of bondage. Open thy mouth wide and I will fill it." When we come to God in need and ask, He fills our mouth with good things. In Matthew 7:11 we are reminded, "If you, then, though you are evil, know how to give good gifts to your children, how much more will your Father in heaven give good gifts to those who ask him."

The good things the Lord gives to us can be found in His Word. They are not necessarily material things, though material things are a part of the package. James says they are "good things." In James 1:17 we read, "Every good and perfect gift is from above, coming down from the Father of the heavenly lights, who does not change like shifting shadows." The last time I checked the Word of God, I came to the conclusion that His arms are not too short to provide my needs, nor his ears deaf to hear my requests. He is not slack concerning His promises and those promises found in His Word are yea and amen. I also realized that His love is far reaching and His power is unlimited. Moreover, I discovered that His Word is still true today as it was yesterday and will be true even tomorrow. You and I need to always remember that if the Lord did it before, He can do it again. Let me give you a few examples:

He supplied daily needs ("oil well" from a jar). God did it for the widow of Zarapheth through her encounter with Elijah (I Kings 17:13-16), and He did if for the Widow of Bethel (II Kings 4:1-7) when her husband, a servant of the prophet died and left her in debt. If God provided for them, then He can do it for you today!

He parted the water—an obstacle to entering into their promise. In Exodus 14:21, God parted the water for the children of Israel when Moses was leading them out of Egypt. Again, in Joshua 3:15-16, He did it for Joshua at the Jordan when the river was at its peak. In II Kings 2:8, He parted the water for Elijah after the Man of God struck it with his mantle. He removed the obstacle that was hindering His people from entering into their "Promised Land," and He will do the same for you today. No obstacle before you shall remain standing if you claim the Word of God and have faith in Him. I declare to you that the obstacle you see before you today, it is the last time you will see it in

Jesus' name. Believe it and act in faith. Remember that when you put your faith into action, God goes into motion.

He caused the rapture. The Bible says in Genesis 5:24 that Enoch walked with God and he "was not" because the Lord took him. In II Kings 2:11, Elijah was taken up to heaven by a whirlwind. In Acts 1:9-11, Jesus was taken up to heaven as His disciples looked intently into the sky. He did it for them then: He will do it for us also. In I Thessalonians 4:16-17, we learn that we will be caught up with Him in the air when the trumpet sounds and the dead in Christ will rise. I cannot wait to see that happen. What a glorious day and sight it will be! The day when all our troubles will be over. The day when this mortal body shall take on immortality and we will be able to sit at the feet of our Lord in total awe of His magnificent power and splendor.

It is therefore fair to conclude that God has continued to prove over the ages that He is not limited by time, space, or circumstances. He will not fail us because His compassion fails not (Lamentation 3:22). God asked the Prophet Isaiah a rhetorical question that is mindboggling. He questioned the Prophet in Isaiah 49:15, "Can a mother forget the baby at her breast and have no compassion on the child she has borne? Though she may forget, I will not forget you!" What a promise! God is saying to you, "I WILL NOT FORGET YOU!" This is a promise that you can take to the bank. The God who controls the universe made this promise to Isaiah and is making the same promise to you today. That is why He provides good things. In our sickness, He heals. That is why He is called Jehovah Rapha, the One who heals (Exodus 15:26). When we lack the daily necessities of life, He provides. That is why He is called Jehovah Jireh, the One who provides our needs (Genesis 22:12-14). The name Jehovah Jireh literally means, "The Lord Who Sees", or "The Lord Who Will See To It." We long for such a provider when we have a need that is personal and special; the One who will see to our needs and provide for us. This is what Jehovah-Jireh means; the Lord Who will see to it that my every need is met. He is the One who knows my needs because He can see them. He is the One who is able to meet my needs at just the right time as He did for Abraham, and the One who can meet them fully. For Abraham, it was the ram caught in the thicket, offered in Isaac's place. For us, it could be whatever we need. Like the eagle parents, the Lord provides good things for His children.

I must point out another fact about eaglets that is applicable to human babies. It is the fact that eaglets do not just eat anything. They eat "eagle food." They have a diet that enables them to grow, mature and become strong. Without a proper diet, the eaglets will become sick, weak and may eventually die. When we have babies, we feed them with breast milk and other baby formulas for a while and then gradually, we introduce cereal and other semi-solid food. After the baby reaches a certain age, we then begin to give them food that adults consume. Any attempt to give a one week old baby adult food could lead to the child's life being cut short. Eagles are also aware of that and take care in giving their babies the right kind of food. But allow me to use an analogy involving us (adults) as God's eaglets if I may from a spiritual perspective.

Just as little babies and eaglets have special diet, we as God's children, (God's eaglets if you will), have a diet (eagle's food) that we should feast upon or else we run the risk of cutting short our spiritual life. That diet is nothing else but the Word of God. We need it to grow and to become strong and mature in the Lord. If not, we become weak spiritually and when attacked by the enemy, we could be defeated. Isaiah 55:2 asks this question "Why spend money on what is not bread, and your labor on what does not satisfy? Listen, listen to me, and eat what is good, and your soul will delight in the richest of fare." When tempted by the devil in Matthew 4:1-11, one of Jesus' replies to the devil when asked to turn stones into bread was that man does not live on bread alone but from every word that comes from the mouth of the LORD (Deuteronomy 8:3). This was the instruction that God gave to the children of Israel regarding the manna with which He fed them. It was a reminder to them that their survival was not dependent upon bread alone but by the very words spoken by the Lord. In Deuteronomy 8:3, the word, "every" signifies all of God's word and not just some. We are to feast on all of God's words in order to grow, develop, mature and remain fruitful. In Psalms 119:160a, we are told, "All your words are true." Paul writes in II Timothy 3:16-17, that "All Scripture is God-breathed and is useful for teaching, rebuking, correcting and training in righteousness, so that the man of God may be thoroughly equipped for every good work."

When eaglets hatch, they are provided with everything they need in order to survive. They do not find themselves homeless or living in a shelter. They do not find their parents about to be kicked out of their home or apartment because they did not take time to prepare for their arrival. They do not encounter their parents going through divorce and find themselves caught in the midst of a fierce child-custody battle. Instead, they calmly open their eyes to a comfortable nest prepared high up on the rocky crags, secured and safe from all predators. Snuggled under the parent's protecting wings, every move of the young ones is watched. Their parents supply all of their needs. In other words, the young eaglets soon discover that life is good. Mom and dad did their homework. They are loved, blessed, appreciated and well taken care of. Whenever they open their mouths, food is waiting to be dropped into them. Obviously, the little eaglets will want to stay in the nest forever. Life is safe and easy. The nest is so cozy and so comfortable. Who would not want to live such an easy life?

Within a few weeks, the eaglets begin to notice a change in their body structure. They notice that they are gaining more feathers and becoming stronger and braver. They begin to wonder what is out beyond their nest, and where mom and dad are getting the food. They soon notice that their parents fly away and come back with food. Somehow, it starts to register in their brains that they are meant to fly as well. They are meant to soar the heavenly heights; to breathe the heavenly atmosphere. It is inherent in them. Their very nature demands it. God has placed it there. The eagle predilection is to mount up. The sky beckons them to come; the other birds call out in unison; the wind whispers calm words of reassurance and creates a perfect opportunity to soar the heights above. The eaglets then begin to realize that they are not meant to be earth-bound or nest-bound but are destined to soar the sky.

Exactly as it is with eagles, so it is with Christians, God's spiritual eagles. God desires for us to experience the best the world has to offer and to experience heavenly heights in the spirit. He wants us to spread our wings of faith, take hold of His grace received through Christ, and ride the heavenly winds of the Holy Spirit who is called the *Parakletos* (called to one's side to help). It's inherent in us. Our new nature, as believers, demands it. Father God has placed it within our DNA. As eaglets of God, there is an inborn tendency in us to mount up and soar to spiritual levels we have never experienced before. Paul writes in Colossians 3: 1-2, "If you then be risen with Christ, seek those things which are above. Set your affection on things above."

Where is your heart? What have you set your affection upon? Have you soared lately? Is your mind set on God and on heavenly things or is it set on the things of this earth that will soon pass away? When was the last time you dared to trust God and launched out spiritually into the depths? It is a fact that chickens and eagles are both birds, but a chicken is an earth-bound creature flapping its wings in an attempt to fly, but scarcely able to get its feet off the ground. This is not true of the eagle. You and I are not meant to be chickens but eagles. We are called to be God's eagle Christians, but unfortunately many of us have become complacent and resolved within ourselves to merely live the chicken life, confined to barnyard limitation in our spirit.

A barnyard, for believers, is any attitude, mindset or lifestyle that restricts us from accomplishing or becoming all that God has purposed for us to do or be in life. Our barnyard is that comfort zone where we prefer to live because it makes no demands of us that will challenge us to change. It is that place of complacency, mediocrity, purposeless living, and lack of vision. An eaglet would prefer to stay in its nest and be fed by its parents continuously but this is not what God created eagles to be. Eventually, the parents will begin to teach the eaglet that there is more to life. The eaglet also begins to realize for itself that it is destined to be king of the sky.

The same is true for us. When we start to become very comfortable in our barnyard mentality, Jehovah Father eagle calls upon us from our barnyard and challenges us to spread our wings of faith and mount higher to the next level. Sometimes, even before He calls, we begin to realize that life within the barnyard is not "it", not our final destiny. We know that something is missing. We know that we have not yet arrived at our "Promised Land". There is a yearning; there is an inner search; there is a hope and a dream; there is a baby that needs to be brought forth from our womb; there is a vision that needs to be spelled out; and there is a purpose for your life that is yet to be discovered. We know these things to be true. Yet, we are sometimes afraid to launch out. Even when we hear the call from God through His Spirit, only a few of us are ready to respond immediately and take the leap of faith that it requires. We know that it might necessitate the exploration of the unknown like in the case of Abraham. The Lord told him in Genesis 12:1 to leave his homeland to go to the land that He (God) would show him. But we know the end of the story as well. God led Abraham and blessed him for his obedience. Those who are ready to willingly obey the voice of the Lord without holding back, and step out into the world of the unknown, He honors. They are those who know that God holds the entire universe and the hearts of kings in His hands. The Lord is seeking that group and it is that group with which He is ready to work. That is the group the Lord wants to teach the techniques of how to possess the sky and dominate it. That is the group He calls His eagles. They constitute the first group.

Another group of chickens, or in this case, people, may respond differently. They may take a leap, but one that is only high enough to get them out of the barn and land them on the barnyard fence post. They then try to play it safe by remaining on the fence post because they are not sure what is awaiting them beyond the barnyard. Unfortunately, the view from the barnyard fence post is rather shortsighted; only a view of the nearby grass, trees, animals grazing in the pasture, the old farmhouse with the farmer and his wife. Discouraged, they may be tempted to jump back into their "barn" thinking that, having seen all that life has to offer, it is not very interesting in the outside world. Or, they may decide that the sight is beautiful from the height where they are sitting and therefore there is no need to go back into the barn or jump down from the fence on the other side. Consequently, all they experience is the beauty and not necessarily the fullness of the new world outside the barn.

The third group of chickens hears the call to explore the world outside the barn and choose to ignore it completely. They are perfectly contented with life inside the barn and believe that there is no need to see anything else. They believe, "If God wanted us to be born outside the barn, we would have been. Since He put us here, we will stay where we are." This defeatist mentality has contaminated many of us, persuading us to allow our birthplace, ethnicity, sex, or other existential realities, over which we have no control, to define us. I believe that the Lord is saying to you, as He has on numerous occasions, "That is not who you are. I allowed you to be born in that place, under those conditions for a reason, as a training ground. It is time to move on. You have completed the training. It is time to mount up into the winds and explore the world. The sky is your limit. I set up a divine plan for you." Regrettably, some of us reply, "God, we are happy where we are. We are not stepping out of this barn. We will remain confined in these four walls. It is better to stay with the devil you know then the angel you do not know." Sad, is it not! But, that is exactly how many of us react to the call of God. It saddens His heart to see how we limit the potential He has given to us. Would you not be sad as well if your child behaved that way and you know that he could accomplish so much more, and had the ability to change his destiny? Would you not want to shake, shout, and scream at your child, "Can't you see that you can do better? Can't you see your potential and all that you are able to do with God's help?"

For those who say, "Lord, here I am. What do I need to do to leave this barn?" He smiles and says, "Let the training begin!"

Like any training intended to bring the best out of you, it is not usually a walk in the park or a piece of cake, but it is guaranteed to change your life for the better. Let me explain how He may choose to train us by briefly sharing with you how the parent eagles train their young ones to fly out of their nest into the world of the unknown and soar the skies.

In the first place, the eagles wait until their babies' feathers are fully grown before they begin to "stir the nest." This involves getting rid of everything in the nest that has made it soft and comfortable. It includes the removal of all the animal skins, extra feathers and fur placed there initially when the nest was built to make it comfortable for the baby eaglets. The objective is to make the nest very uncomfortable and miserable to the point where the eaglet will want to get out. The mother eagle is the parent who initiates and is most actively involved in this process: she begins to help her eaglets develop strength in their wings. She teaches them how to flap their wings by doing so herself and they eventually begin to imitate her. As they flap their wings, the eaglets shed their loose feathers that would have hindered them or serve as extra weight when they fly. For the stubborn feathers that remain attached to the eaglets, the mother is pleased to remove them with her beak or by flapping her wings furiously causing a mighty wind to blow upon the eaglets to remove the excess feathers. Think about this for a moment: Mother eagle causing a furious wind to develop as a result of her deliberate action.

The description mentioned above does not sound like fun. Pulling loose feathers can be painful. It is like pulling a loose tooth. It hurts and blood is sometimes shed. Similarly, furious wind can be frightening and dangerous. Yet, it is part of the process in preparing the eaglets to fly. Keep in mind that the mother waited until the eaglet's wings were fully developed. This is key! God will not take you through a test for which you are not ready or allow a storm that you cannot withstand. That is why the psalmist says; "He prepares a table before you in the presence of your enemies." Your enemies are not your friends. Their intention is to cheat, harm, molest, disgrace, and maybe kill you. But, God prepares a sumptuous meal for you and sits you before them. It either means that He has surrounded you with His protection and your enemies cannot touch you or that you are so equipped that you are not afraid of the enemies' plans or it could be both. Whatever the case, you are ready to withstand the onslaught of your enemies. A pastor friend recently reminded his congregation to pray for their enemies because if they pray diligently, they may live long enough to see their enemies attend their anointing service. I found his remark to be fascinating! I may not totally agree with his theology but I found another reason why I need to pray for my enemies; that they will one day attend my anointing service because God has promised to anoint my head with oil in the presence of my enemies.

There are some of you reading this book who can identify with the "stirring of the nest" experience. It is discomforting. Things do not appear to be okay. You know that something is not quite right but you do not know what it is. Deep within, you are convinced that God will see you through but the wind is terrible. It is blinding your sight and you are not sure when it will end. Maybe it is your job or your finances that are shaking. Maybe your marriage is shaking and you are doing everything you can to stabilize the situation but it is just not working. Could it be that God is stirring your nest? Could it be that He is telling you that it is time to get out of your comfort zone? Could it be that He is stirring the water and it is time for you to jump in to get your miracle? Could it be that He is about to take you to that next level but you are too relaxed in your nest? God did not call us as eagles to be nest dwellers or nest sitters all of our lives. He made us to fly and when we do not fly, He has to go the extra mile to help us understand what He wants us to do. It could mean that He will have to begin ripping our nest apart and then creating that furious wind to let us know that where we are is no longer safe or where we need to be and it is time to move on.

Maybe your situation is a little different. Maybe it has to do with "loose feathers" in your life. Maybe it has to do with behaviors or attitudes in your life that are affecting your spiritual progress and are dragging you down. Maybe there are things you know that you should be doing but you are not doing, or vice versa, because of whatever reason best known to you. The Holy Spirit has a way of convicting us and making us uncomfortable. Do not resist what the Spirit of the Lord is doing. It is for your own good. It may appear to be difficult and uncomfortable, but it will be okay.

It is time to quit fluttering around in the nest and to learn how to spread your wings of faith and fly.

Alas, for some of us the "stirring of the nest" is a horrifying experience. Though it is meant to prepare us for greater and better things, we become so frightened that we turn our backs on the process and tell Father Eagle (God in this case) to leave us alone. We find a way either to walk away from our nest or to bury ourselves deeper into it. We detest the process and begin to hurl insults at God. We tell Him how much He does not love us and how much we hate Him. Despondently, we go away from His presence not trusting Him with our lives. Like the rich young man in Matthew 19:16-26, we walk away sad because of all that we are holding onto and do not want to let go. I pray that this does not happen to you. May you be willing for God to get rid of those loose feathers in your life!

After getting rid of all the loose feathers, the parent eagle (usually the mother) spreads out her wings, and with a scream, beckons her eaglet to step forth onto her wings. Although afraid of the sight below and horrified of the thought of falling to its death, the eaglet obeys and steps out in faith, knowing that he can trust his mother and the safety of her wings. When the eaglet has firmly secured itself upon mommy's wing using its talons, he grabs hold of one of mommy's big feathers with its beak. Upon thorough inspection that her eaglet is firmly attached, the mother takes flight into the sky with the little one holding on firmly in fear of his life. In no time, the eaglet begins to enjoy the flight. The fear he initially experienced quickly vanishes as he starts to go places that he has never been before and see things he has never seen before. "This isn't bad after all!" He begins to think to himself. Maybe he even asks his mother, "Why didn't we do this a long time ago?"

Surprisingly, what appears to be fun now for the eaglet soon becomes a nightmare and a desperate plea for help. After a short flight time, the mother eagle begins to flutter her wings and suddenly shakes the eaglet loose from her wing. She does this unexpectedly and briskly, hundreds of feet high in the air. In shock, the eaglet begins tumbling down out of the sky and likely begins to say to itself, "I knew that my mom and dad did not like me in the first place. If they wanted me dead, why didn't they just tell me? Look at how I am going to die such a miserable death. By the time I hit the ground below, there will be nothing left of me. Why is this happening to me?" What is even more surprising to the eaglet is that while he is apparently "falling to its death," his mother is "uselessly" circling above him. His mother is merely keeping a watchful eye on him, but refusing to intervene. In fact, his mother seems to be telling it to do something, but how can he pay attention while experiencing a rapid free fall from the sky? Meanwhile, the eaglet says to himself as he flounders, flutters, and somersaults, trying to fly for the first time, "I can make it; I know that I can!" Unfortunately, even while the eaglet makes those declarations, he realizes that he is losing altitude. At this point, he is dangerously close to the ground and he says, "I am finished!" It is at that very moment that the mother eagle swoops down, snares her baby with a taloned claw and flies him into the sky to restart the process. Depending on the emotional state of the eaglet, the mother may return him to his nest and repeat the training the next day or continue the training the same day. Each day the training continues until the little eagle learns how to stay aloft riding the air currents, soaring as effortlessly as the parent eagles do.

If you are like me, you are probably wondering, "Where is the father and why isn't he a part of the process?" The answer to this interesting question is, the father was nearby all along, flying around, patrolling for predators who might want to tamper with the training process or feast on his vulnerable child. The father was closely watching all that was happening and will fight any bird to the death that entered his territory.

The eagle has an enemy called the condor. This bird believes it should be the king of the sky and consequently hates the eagle. Interestingly, condors are the largest flying land birds in the Western Hemisphere. They are also known to be the world's heaviest flying bird. Some of them weigh over 25 pounds and have a wingspan of approximately 10 feet. Given the fact that the condor hates the eagle, the latter has to be on the lookout at all times for its enemy, especially when its young ones are being trained. When challenged to a fight, the eagle does not generally fight the condor. It usually mounts up and begins to fly toward the sun. God has blessed the eagle with a special eyelid that filters the sun's rays, so to evade a condor, the eagle simply flies directly toward the sun and, as the condor tries to catch the eagle, it soon is blinded by the sun's rays and is forced to turn back from its pursuit of the eagle. Allow me point out as well that if the male eagle sees that its baby is being threatened by the condor, it will not fly towards the sun or run away. It will stay and fight its enemy who is stronger, larger and heavier even if it would cost the male eagle to lose his life.

Do you remember the test or courtship process the male eagle went through before its marriage? The first stage was for the male eagle to catch a twig before it falls to the ground. It is at this time that the father is expected to put that skill into practice. Just in case the mother misses the eaglet while it is falling, the father is expected to swiftly scoop up the eaglet before it hits the ground.

Several poignant spiritual truths can be gleaned from the flight training of an eaglet. The first is found in the way the mother eagle spreads her wings and commands her eaglets to step out in faith on them, taking hold of a feather with its beak. Typologically, the two wings of the parent eagle can be likened to how we must "stand" upon both the Old and the New Testaments together forming the Word of God. The feathers can be thought of as the individual promises found in the Word of God. In other words, God as our Father eagle spreads His Word before us (the two wings) and commands us to step out on it; our task is to firmly grasp the promises found therein. There are many promises God has made to us that are found in His holy Word. Look at a few of these incredible promises:

1) For I know the plans I have for you, declares the Lord, "plans to prosper you and not to harm you, plans to give you hope and a future" (Jeremiah 29:11).
2) Come to me, all you who are weary and burdened, and I will give you rest. Take my yoke upon you and learn from me, for I am gentle and humble in heart, and you will find rest for your souls (Matthew 11:28-29).

3) And this same God who takes care of me will supply all your needs from His glorious riches, which have been given to us in Christ Jesus (Philippians 4:19).

4) No, in all these things we are more than conquerors through Him who loved us *(Romans 8:37).*

5) But whoever listens to me will live in safety and be at ease, without fear of harm *(Proverbs 1:33).*

6) I am leaving you with a gift—Peace of mind and heart. The peace I give is a gift the world cannot give. So do not be troubled or afraid *(John 14:27).*

7) If you declare with your mouth, Jesus is Lord, and believe in your heart that God raised Him from the dead, you will be saved *(Romans 10:9).*

8) For the revelation awaits an appointed time; it speaks of the end and will not prove false. Though it lingers, wait for it; it will certainly come and will not delay (Habakkuk 2:3).

What more is there to ask of God? His promises are not empty—far from it! All of heaven backs God's promises. Just as the eaglet experiences an unexpected shaking that causes it to lose its hold on mother eagle's feathers, we may encounter a severe "shaking" in our lives as well, but it does not mean God's promises are not true. On the contrary, during challenging times we must hold onto them even more firmly. We, as God's eaglets, undergo "shaking" times, but that shaking is not unto death. Never let go of God's promises when you are subjected to a shaking. Do not become despondent! Do not get frustrated! Do not throw in the towel. It is all part of the training process. If you want to learn how to fly, you must submit to the process. You may be falling, but God will not let you hit the ground. He will rescue you!

It is vital that an eagle learns how to fly. It is a matter of survival. Learning how to fly determines the extent to which an eagle will maximize its full potential in exploring the unknown world. The same is true for the Christian. "Flying" for a believer is not used in this context to mean moving through the air by means of wings, aircraft or spacecraft. Rather, it is used in the context of moving swiftly and skillfully to escape the attack of the enemy and to accomplish God's plan. It could also refer to the act of experiencing joy, peace and happiness in the midst of a tumultuous situation. The Christian must remember that in the midst of trials and tribulations, God is able to either calm the storm or calm His child. When He chooses to calm His child, God provides her the ability to "fly above" the situation. It may appear that all else is crumbling around the Christian, but this "eaglet" that has learned to fly as an eagle will not be touched. Everything else may be crumbling around the one who has learned how to fly as an eagle, but he or she will not be touched. The Bible declares in Psalms 91:7 "A thousand may fall at your side, ten thousand at your right hand, but it will not come near you." The reason why defeat will not come near you is because Christ is with you and you have learned how to "fly." The Spirit of God, which resides within you, provides the ability to duck the arrows that the enemy points at you.

It is important to keep in mind that the parent eagles do not abandon their eaglet during the training process. They are watching. In the same way, God never abandons us. Even when we are shaking, flustered, disoriented, and frustrated during a period of trials and tribulations, He never lets us hit the ground. Similarly, as the eagle parents continue to instruct their young until they are fully trained, so our Father God continues to work with us, His children, never giving up on us in spite of all our mistakes and failures. We can count on Philippians 1:6, " . . . He who began a good work in you will carry it on to completion . . ."

We have explained how God will not abandon you. We also explained how God is faithful in keeping His promises made to you. But, here are some questions worth pondering: Are you faithful in keeping the promises you made to God, yourself and your family? Can your spouse, children and other family members count on you, or do you abandon them when the going gets rough? Are you willing to step out in faith when the Lord beckons you to follow Him? Are you able to step out of your boat, as Peter did, in order to walk on water into Jesus' outstretched arms? I hope you are able to answer "yes" to all these questions. If not, pray that the Lord will help you!

CHAPTER VI

UNDERSTANDING HOW TO RULE
AS AN EAGLE

"But, ask the animals, and they will teach you,
or the birds of the air, and they will tell you;
or speak to the earth, and it will teach you,
or let the fish of the sea inform you.
Which of all these does not know that the
Lord has done this?" (Job 12:7-9)

The psalmist posed a profound question in Psalms 8:4-7. He asked, "What is man that you are mindful of him, the son of man that you care for him? You made him a little lower than the heavenly beings and crowned him with glory and honor. You made him ruler over the works of your hands; you put everything under his feet." When we are able to answer this question in the light of God's over-all plan for mankind, then we will be in the position to fully understand and appreciate why and how we should rule as God's eagles.

When God made Adam and Eve and placed them in the Garden of Eden, He had great plans for them. God's desire was for them to experience nothing but the best this life had to offer. He created them to enjoy His blessings. Ponder over the creation story for a moment. You will quickly realize that it was God who planted the Garden without man's help. It was God's decision, not Adam and Eve's request, that landed them there. God offered both Adam and Eve free food from all the trees (save one) without them needing to beg Him for food. In other words, Adam did not plow the ground, did not plant the trees, did not water them, and he probably did not prune them either. He simply enjoyed them. You will notice also that God's first command to mankind (Genesis 1:28) was not for him to tend the garden but to have dominion over the earth. God instructed, "Be fruitful and increase in number; fill the earth and subdue it. Rule over the fish of the sea and the birds of the air and over every living creature that moves on the ground." Everything man needed for survival, God had already made available. Hence, it was not necessary for Adam to expend manual labor and work for his daily bread in order to survive. All God asked was for man to serve as His steward over creation. Consequently, He gave man these five instructions: 1) Be fruitful; 2) Increase in number; 3) Fill the earth; 4) Subdue the earth; 5) Rule over creatures in the air and on the ground.

In His divine wisdom, God established man as the ruler over all His creation. Given the fact that God is the supreme Ruler and Creator, He had the authority to hand over His creation to whomever He wished, and He chose to turn it over to mankind. By so doing, He made man His co-ruler and co-creator. Man became co-ruler by virtue of the fact that God asked man to rule over the earth and co-creator because God gave mankind the ability to reproduce and replenish. God knew exactly what He was doing when He put man in charge of the earth; He knew what He was doing and why He was doing it. When God was about to create mankind, He decided, "Let us make man in our image and likeness" (Genesis 1:26). Thus, mankind had been created in the image of God. This means, among many things, that God has equipped us to rule over the rest of His creation effectively and efficiently. In some way, we, His creatures and handiwork, resemble the Creator. God has chosen to image Himself to the world by means of mankind. Like God, we have a spirit (cf. John 4:23-24); we have a free will (cf. Joshua 24:14-15); we have a moral dimension (cf. Ephesians 4:24); we have a rational nature; and we have the drive to dominate or a dominion nature. When analyzing the God-given nature that man possesses and the authority that God has given to him on the earth, the psalmist asked, "What is mankind that you are mindful of them, human beings that you care for them? You have made them **a little lower** than the angels and **crowned them** with **glory and honor**. You made them rulers over the works of your hands; you put **everything under their feet**" (Psalms 8:4-6—emphasis is mine). It is therefore indisputable that God intended for us to rule not only here on earth in this life, but also in heaven in the life to come. Paul tells the church in Corinth that saints of God will judge this world and angels as well (I Corinthians 6:2-3). What a wonderful privilege God extends to us! Can you picture yourself judging angels? Think about it for a second and read about the archangel Michael whose name means "Who is like unto God?" (Daniel 10:21; 1 Thessalonians 4:16; Jude 9; Revelation 12:7). Or ponder the archangel Gabriel, whose name means "Hero of God" (Daniel 8:16; 9:21; Luke 1:18-19; 26-38). Even though some biblical scholars believe we will only judge fallen angels, just the same, the thought of judging any angel (fallen or pure) is beyond my wildest imagination. The Bible says that you will judge cherubim that are tasked with defending God's holiness from any defilement of sin (Genesis 3:24; Exodus 20 and Ezekiel 1:1-18) and seraphim that have three pairs of wings (Isaiah 6:2-7) whose primary functions are praising God and being His messengers to earth. Wow, this is heavy-duty stuff! I admit that I cannot imagine cognitively how I could judge angels that defend God's holiness and righteousness and even those whose spend countless hours praising the

Lord! Thanks be to God for His grace—that unmerited, unearned, and undeserved favor He has bestowed upon us because of what Christ did for us on the cross. Some biblical scholars have defined grace as "**G**od's **R**iches **A**t **C**hrist's **E**xpense." I guess that is where the doctrine of propitiation[48] comes in as well. Thank God for His grace!

I think it would be acceptable and understandable for Christians to have differences of opinion regarding how God intends human to rule over the earth (our stewardship responsibilities and personal roles), but it would be impossible for anyone to convince me that God did **not** intend for us to govern this earth. For those who disagree with the assertion that God wants us to have dominion over the earth, I would redirect them to look at the "bigger picture" and reread the Bible.

There is an old fable, originating in India, about six men, blind from birth, who visited a nearby palace. When they arrived, there was an elephant standing in the courtyard. The men decided to examine the elephant and concluded about what an elephant looks like. The first blind man touched the side of the

---

[48] Propitiation is the doctrine that the person and death of Jesus Christ appeases God's wrath and satisfies His holiness, meeting the righteous demands of God, thereby enabling the sinner to be reconciled unto Him.

elephant and said, "An elephant is like a wall." The second blind man touched the trunk and said, "An elephant is like a snake." The third blind man touched the tusk and said, "An elephant is like a spear." The fourth blind man touched the leg and said, "An elephant is like a tree." The fifth blind man touched the ear and said, "An elephant is like a fan." The sixth blind man touched the tail and said, "An elephant is like a rope." Because each blind man touched only one part of the elephant, they could not come to a consensus on the elephant's appearance. Karen Backstein in her book, "*The blind men and the elephant*" writes, "The elephant is a very large animal. Its side is like a wall. Its trunk is like a snake. Its tusks are like spears. Its legs are like trees. Its ears are like fans. And its tail is like a rope. So you are all right. But, you are all wrong, too. For each of you touched only one part of the animal. To know what an elephant is really like, you must put all those parts together."[49] The same is applicable to us regarding how God has called us to rule on earth and the territory over which he wants us to have dominion.

To assist us in clearly understanding how He wants us to rule as Eagle Christians, we will again consider the life of an eagle. Our first consideration is called imprinting.

---

[49] Backstein, Karen. *The Blind Men and the Elephant*. New York: Scholastic, 1992.

It may surprise you to know that although eagles are excellent hunters and perfectly suited to flight, they still must be taught how to hunt and fly. These abilities do not appear spontaneously just because they are eagles. Eagles must be willing to learn and intentionally taught.

I have a few students that I am currently teaching how to play the keyboard, guitar and drums. Some of them are gifted musically, I have no doubt. For those who are naturally gifted musically, learning how to play a musical instrument comes easily and naturally but they still have to be willing to learn and they must be taught. Yet, for a few of my students, it is a struggle. They need extra time and attention. In fact, I jokingly told one of them recently, "You are determined to make me a failure in teaching someone how to play the guitar." He remarked: "Doc, I am doing my best, trust me." I knew he was and I felt sympathy for him. In any case, for my students to succeed, they must first of all be motivated to learn and willing to be taught. There is an old proverb that says, "You can lead a horse to water, but you can't make him drink." In other words, God has given us the ability to rule but He will not force us to. For some people, ruling comes naturally, whereas for others, it requires a little more effort.

Whatever the situation, applying the principle of dominion begins when we submit to the process called imprinting. This form of learning occurs when a young animal fixes its attention upon the first object with which it has visual, auditory, or tactile experience and thereafter follows that object. This bonding experience takes place in birds when they come out of their eggs. They instantly bond with the first moving object they see. For example, if a chicken hatches an eagle's egg, the eaglet will immediately bond with the hen and will begin to see the hen as its mother. It will begin to behave like the hen even though it is an eagle, possessing abilities that are superior to those of chickens. The eaglet will observe and imitate the hen and other chicks around it. If the eaglet is not quickly recognized and rescued by a flying eagle, he will eventually grow up to be an eagle behaving like a chicken.

The concept of imprinting does not just stop with observing and imitating, it is even deeper and fascinating. If you talk to experts at bird shelters who rescue eagle eggs, they will tell you that they use eagle puppets when feeding eaglets to avoid the young birds' imprinting on humans. If baby eaglets do not imprint on the visual appearance of eagles, later on they will resist their own kind when it is time to partner and begin a family.

As God's creatures, we have this imprinting nature within us as well. Although we were created in the image of God, we were born in sin, and sin continues to corrupt our lives. The psalmist declares in Psalms 51:5, "Surely I was sinful at birth, sinful from the time my mother conceived me." Not only were we born with a sinful nature, we were also born into a sinful world. Consequentially, our imprinting nature led us down the path in the direction of sin without any effort on our part. Therefore, we are inclined to want to sin and find pleasure in it. In desperation, Jeremiah, after observing the deprivation of man's heart cried out, "The heart is deceitful above all things and beyond cure. Who can understand it?"[50]

I had the opportunity to witness the first year of the Liberian civil war in West Africa. During those dark days I came to understand the magnitude of wickedness of which man is capable. I saw young children from good homes join the rebel forces and begin killing innocent civilians displaying their severed heads and intestines as trophies on cars or at checkpoints. I was terrified beyond words and could not believe what I saw daily. That same sinful nature resides in us, even when we are saved by the God's grace as a result of Christ's work on the cross. Paul explains in Romans chapter seven that there is a "war" that is raging in us. If we are conflicted within ourselves about how to act, then

---

[50] Jeremiah 17:9

how can we know how to rule God's world properly? We must not trust our own sinful inclinations, but instead faithfully follow our Supreme Ruler and Creator. Paul writes in I Corinthians 11:1, "Imitate me, just as I also imitate Christ." We are to follow the Master's voice, follow the Master's plan, and follow the Master's lead. That is the first step in understanding how to rule as an eagle: "Imprinting" onto Christ. We must know the Master's voice, and follow it. Jesus said, "My sheep listen to my voice; I know them and they follow me" (John 10:27). In order to "know His voice," we must first know Him. It comes from having a relationship with Him through His Son, Jesus Christ. The more we get to know Jesus through the reading of the Bible, prayer, hearing the Word preached, and fellowshipping with other believers, the more we will get to know the Father because Jesus said, "I and the Father are one" (John 10:30).

The second step in preparation for ruling is to be willing to learn and submit to the teaching process. In order for eaglets to learn to fly, hunt and soar the sky, they must submit themselves to the voices, plans and examples of their parents. Eaglets submit to the teaching process when it comes to eating. At first, the parents feed the eaglets but eventually, the eaglets must find food for themselves. This does not happen automatically; the eaglet must be taught and be willing to learn the techniques. Likewise with flying; an eaglet does not wake up one day and say, "I am an eagle, I can fly, and here I go!" If it does that, he would fall to his death. He must submit to the learning process.

In proverbs 22:6 we are admonished to train up our children in the way they should go, so that when they are old, they will not depart from it. As God teaches us, His children, He expects us to teach our children as well. Just like the mother eagle, our Father takes us through various stages of learning in order to perfect the nature He has placed within us. These stages are:

1) The **Demonstrating** Stage: A parent eagle demonstrates to the eaglet how to fly by hovering over the nest. The eaglet learns by watching the parent eagle. God has demonstrated His love towards us (Romans 5:8) through Christ. Paul said to Timothy, "And yet for this reason I found mercy, in order that in me as the foremost, Jesus Christ might demonstrate His perfect patience, as an example for those who believe in Him for eternal life" (I Timothy 1:16). Jesus is our living demonstration of God's love.

2) The **Discomforting** Stage: the parent eagle makes the eaglet uncomfortable in the nest when the time has come for it to learn how to fly. The parent does so by "stirring up" the nest. The young eaglet is literally forced out of its comfortable nest. God sometimes does the same to us. We become uneasy, troubled,

restless, or directionless. Job said, "My heart is troubled and restless . . ." (Job 30:27). We may experience restlessness from a broken relationship, stress at work, or weakness in the body. God may be allowing these times as an indication that it is time for us to move on.

3) The **Dangerous** Stage: It becomes dangerous for the eaglet that chooses to ignore the mother's voice to get out of its nest. The mother would continue to rip up the nest until there is virtually nothing left. In our lives, God may allow a distressing situation to escalate when we are ignoring His warning or call to move on. We may become seriously sick, loose a job, or our spouse may run off with someone else. Suddenly we realize that we need to act fast because the situation is becoming increasingly dangerous. Psalms 119:67 reads, "Before I was afflicted I went astray, but now I obey your word." It seems King David had to experience an affliction in order to obey the Word of God.

4) The **Deciding** Stage: At this stage, an eaglet realizes it has only two options: to fly and live, or to fall and die. It is the same with us; we each must decide whether we will trust and obey God or curse Him; if we will run to Him or run away from Him. We will succumb to a free fall if we decide not to "fly" with God. Time is of the essence. In Deuteronomy 30:19, God said to the Children of Israel, "This day I call heaven and earth as witnesses against you

that I have set before you life and death, blessings and curses. Now choose life, so that you and your children may live."

5) The **Doing** Stage: This is the final stage for the eaglet. It is time for the eaglet to fly for itself. The same principle applies to us as we learn to "fly" with Christ. It is time to DO what the Lord has directed. If God wants us to repent, then repent. If God wants us to step out in faith, then move out and let God lead the way. Each Christian must "fly solo" because at this stage, no one can "fly" for you. Galatians 6:5 says, "For each one should carry his own load." This does not mean that God abandons us at this time. Far from it! As we are obeying, if we begin to fall, God comes to our rescue as an eagle parent would when his eaglet is falling toward the ground. We must try, move, obey, trust and *then* God will help. The children of Israel had to obey and allow their feet to touch the water of the Jordon River and *then* it parted (Joshua, chapters 3 & 4). In Luke 17:14, when Jesus told the lepers to present themselves to the priest, they were not yet cleansed. As they obeyed and went, their healing took place. A wise person once said, "When faith goes into action, God gets into motion."

Are you at the stage where you believe that God is teaching you how to fly? Have you experienced any of the stages mentioned above? Are you cooperating with God or are you rebelling against Him? Is your attitude right or is it wrong? Are you ready for your "solo" lesson?

As you grow in the Lord (as your "feathers" get stronger), He will begin to "stir the nest." When He begins to push you out of your nest, just remember that it is for your good and that He will never abandon you in the midst of your "flight school."

The third step in beginning to rule as an eagle is to obtain a wise mentor and allow yourself to be taught. The word, "mentor" cannot be found in the Bible. In fact, mentors take their name from a mystical character in Homer's ancient Greek epic poetry. Mentor was a soldier and friend of the hero Odysseus. But actually "he" was a "she"—the goddess Athena in disguise. She assumed Mentor's form to help Odysseus and his family through a variety of tests and trials. While we as Christians reject pagan religions, we can profit from the universal truths contained in ancient myths. The universal truth is that we can gain divine guidance through an older and wiser friend: and that is the simple definition of a mentor.

Although the word "mentor" is not found in the Bible, the concept is surely present. Paul writes to the church in Thessalonica, " . . . Just as a nursing mother cares for her children, so we cared for you. Because we loved you as well, we were delighted to share with you not only the gospel of God but our lives as well" (1 Thessalonians 2:7b-8). Paul makes it clear that this sharing is more than a spiritual relationship, but is affectionate and nurturing, aiming toward holistic success in the life of the mentee.

In most instances, a mentor-mentee relationship is initiated by a more experienced person who wishes to help a younger or less experienced person develop personally, spiritually, or professionally. In the words of John Mallison, "It is a dynamic relationship of trust in which one person enables another to maximize the grace of God in his/her life and service."[51] Dr. J. Robert Clinton says, "Mentoring is one person helping another person to grow. This happens as the mentor transfers resources to the mentee, including knowledge, skills, and networking."[52] A mentor-mentee relationship includes the aspects of guidance, support, protection and role modeling.

In the Bible, we can find many examples of a mentor-mentee relationship, namely: Jesus and His disciples, Barnabas and Paul, Naomi and Ruth, Elijah

---

[51] John Mallison, *Mentoring to Develop Disciples and Leaders,* Scripture Union, NSW, Australia, p. 34

[52] J. Robert Clinton, Mentoring: *Developing Leaders Through Empowering Relationships.*" Lecture at Calvin Seminary. Grand Rapids, Mich., Sept. 1998. Altadena, CA: Barnabas Publisher, pp. 3-4.

and Elisha, Moses and Joshua, Deborah and Barak, just to name a few.

Sometimes finding a mentor is not a formal process where there is a memorandum of understanding or a mutual agreement between the mentor and mentee. Often, it develops naturally as in a mother-daughter or a father-son relationship. Other times, one has to be intentional in identifying an individual who has the skills and abilities needed to serve as a mentor. The point that I am trying to make is that a mentor-mentee relationship should be dynamic and to a certain extent, reciprocal.

Even though there are no set rules, there are few things, in my view, that should characterize this relationship and goals a mentor should try to accomplish. First, a mentor must be concerned about the mentee, with a sincere desire to help. Secondly, a mentor must have the ability to share wisdom, skills, and experiences with the mentee through modeling, coaching and leading. Thirdly, a mentor must be willing and able to constructively correct a mentee when he does something that is inappropriate or steps out of line. Fourthly, a mentor should guide his mentee in developing meaningful relationships (human and spiritual), which will optimize his potential. Finally, a mentor should have the wisdom to know when the time is right to step aside and allow his mentee to "fly" on his own.

Another way of explaining the mentoring process is to understand these six steps, namely:

1) **Tell**: The mentor should be able to tell the mentee what to do and why it must be done.
2) **Show**: The mentor must be able to show how to do it.
3) **Share**: the mentor must share responsibility with the mentee based on his ability.
4) **Watch**: The mentor must step back and watch the mentee execute an assigned task.
5) **Release**: The mentor, at the appropriate time, should release the mentee to fulfill God's ordained calling of life and ministry.
6) **Follow-up**: the mentor should continue to check in with the mentee periodically to offer on-going support, encouragement, feedback and re-direction.

Allow me to illustrate the progression of the mentor-mentee relationship by using the relationship between Barnabas and Paul. When Paul became physically blind on the road to Damascus, the experience also left him blind as to the general direction of his life. Paul had no plan and no support group. Those in Christian circles feared him. He had no one to sympathize and aid him with his situation. He was in desperate need of a mentor. God answered this need by providing Barnabas, whose name means "encourager". From reading the book of Acts we discover: a) Barnabas took the initiative and befriended Paul (Acts 9:26-27); b) Barnabas went to Tarsus and took Paul "under his wings" to Antioch. In Antioch, they lived together for a year teaching the Word of God (Acts 11:22-26); c) Barnabas modeled for Paul how to set up a leadership team for the purpose of prayer, fasting and decision-making. It resulted in the Lord speaking to the group (Acts 13:1-3); d) After Barnabas recognized that his mentee, Paul, had developed the necessary leadership skills, Barnabas stepped aside and moved Paul to the forefront of leadership. Instead of reading, "Barnabas and Saul" (Acts 13:7), we read, "Paul and his companions" (Acts 13:13); d) Barnabas and Paul formed a team in defending Gentile believers before the Jerusalem Council (Acts 15:1-4, 12); e) Barnabas provided on-going guidance by correcting Paul over a negative attitude he held toward a younger Christian brother called John Mark (Acts 15:36-38). Later, Paul admitted indirectly that his mentor, Barnabas was right when he wrote in II Timothy 4:11, "Only Luke is with me. Get Mark and bring him with you, because he is helpful to me in my ministry."

In the Bible, we discover several metaphorical descriptions of a mentor: They are:

a) A Shepherd (1 Peter 4:1-4);
b) A Builder (1 Corinthians 3:10;
c) An Administrator (1 Corinthians 12:28);

d) An Encourager (Acts 11:23; 14:22; Hebrews 3:13);

e) A Gardener or a farmer (Mark 4:26-32; Mark 4:1-20; Luke 8:5-15).

In a mentor-mentee relationship, the mentor teaches, encourages and shows the mentee how to "fly" as an eagle. The mentor helps the mentee navigate the labyrinths of life. The mentor serves as a helpful tour guide, friend, confidante, and encourager, while at the same time rebuking, correcting, and chastening in love. This is exactly what happens in an eagle-eaglet relationship.

The fourth step in understanding how to rule as an eagle is to make an honest appraisal of yourself; your strengths, weaknesses and areas for potential growth. In order to know yourself, you must answer four basic questions of life, namely: a) Who am I? b) What are my choices? c) What is of most importance to me? d) What are my goals in life?

In Hebrews 11:23-29, we read about Moses, the one whom God chose to lead His people out of Egypt, a land of bondage, into the Promised Land. Moses had to wrestle with the four questions mentioned above in order to understand how to "fly as an eagle." First of all, he had to settle the question of his identity. As a Hebrew infant, he was adopted by Pharaoh's daughter and raised as an Egyptian Prince. It was logical for him to undergo an identity crisis and question, "Who am I?" Should I claim my Egyptian identity, forget my heritage and enjoy a life of ease? Should I revert to my Jewish heritage, knowing that I will be humiliated and kicked out of the palace? Moses made his fateful choice and "refused" to be known as the son of Pharaoh's daughter. Consequently, he chose to be mistreated along with the people of God rather than to enjoy the fleeting pleasures of sin (Hebrews 11:24-25). Moses made his choice and you must do the same. As you prepare to rule, you must select the kingdom within which you want to rule, and with whom you are going to rule.

Secondly, Moses took responsibility for his destiny through the choices he made. Moses rejected his Egyptian identity and chose to take up his divine calling as a Hebrew (Hebrews 11:24-25). Though Moses was born into his calling, when he grew up he had to choose God's way for himself. The same is true for us. Though God chose us before the foundation of the world and wants to have a relationship with us, at a certain point in our lives, it is incumbent upon us to take responsibility for our future. You are ultimately responsible for how your life turns out. No one, not even Satan, can ruin your life; Satan has no right to harm you, but you can destroy yourself. Though God loves you, and it would pain Him to watch you become the prey of the devil, ultimately the decision is yours. God is willing and ready to work with you but you have to choose Him. Your happiness is largely determined by the character qualities you exhibit; and your character is formed by the choices you make.

Thirdly, Moses had to honestly ask himself, "What is of most importance to me?" Before addressing that question, one has to establish a value system. This is not a haphazard decision, but requires serious thought. You have to give it serious thought. Moses clarified his values. He thought it out. Moses ***regarded*** disgrace for the sake of Christ as a greater value than the treasures of Egypt, for his value system caused him to look ahead at the "big picture" (Hebrews 11:26). The word "regarded" literally means, "to weigh in the balance, consider the options, evaluate the worth, or consider the value." He concluded that God was greater in value than all of the treasures of Egypt.

What do you value most in life? What is of most importance to you? It is essential that you clearly define your values in life. This is vital because your values influence your stress level, control your success, and affect your salvation and the depth of your relationship with God. Therefore, in order to understand how to rule as an eagle, you must establish a value system you will pattern your life around, and to which you will allow others to hold you accountable. You must:

a) *clarify* what is of most importance to you in life;
b) *choose* the source of your values. In other words, where do you get your values from: television, your political leaders, the Church, the Bible?;
c) *change* your lifestyle and;
d) *check* yourself daily to find out if you are continuing to say and do what you value most.

Both the eaglet and the child of God must set their standard of values above the mediocrity surrounding them. Both must seek to fulfill a higher standard. The people of this world have three common values: a) pleasure—I want to feel good; b) possessions—I want to have a lot; c) power—I want to be famous, popular or influential. Moses decided that God's purpose was more valuable than popularity, God's people were more valuable than pleasures, and God's peace was more valuable than possessions. What is crucial to keep in mind is that Moses' decision was predicated on the fact that he was looking ahead to the future for a reward (Hebrews 11:26b). Jesus said that a man's life does not consist of the abundance of things that he possesses (Luke 12:15). Yet, many of us live as if that is true. Wealth is neutral in and of itself, but our attitude and use of wealth is of great importance. Please stop and honestly evaluate what is of most importance to you.

You don't know? All you have to do is observe where it is you invest your time, talent and resources.

The fourth step is to set goals in life and never take your eyes off those goals. Moses continually focused his attention on the goals that he had set. In Hebrews 11:27, we read that Moses, by faith, left Egypt not fearing the king's anger; he persevered because he saw Him who is invisible. It was necessary for Moses to be persistent; his goals were enormous and humanly impossible. Moses' first goal was to convince the people of God that he was sent by God. Secondly, Moses had to convince a wicked Pharaoh, who feared neither God nor man, to let his free, slave labor walk off the job in Egypt. Thirdly, Moses had to figure out a way to get over two million Hebrews, without plane or ship or train, without food and water, transported from Egypt to the Promised Land. Since he was a young man, Moses knew he was a Hebrew, adopted into a royal Egyptian family, destined to deliver the people of God from the land of bondage, but it took 80 years to convert the vision into action. I am sure that many times he went before the Lord in prayer and said: "Lord, it is me, Moses. Is it time yet?" To his question the Lord would reply, "No, not yet Moses." Waiting can be painful, agonizing, discouraging, irritating and disheartening. Nevertheless, one needs to remain focused on the plan. Delay does not mean denial. God is always working things out. At the right time, He will give the signal. Moses, it seems, had forgotten about his God-given vision. When the Lord called to Moses from a burning bush (Exodus 3), he seemed unprepared and unwilling. Understanding how to fly as an eagle requires patience. Your feathers have to grow. The daddy eagle (God) knows when you are ready and He will let you know. Never take your eyes off the goal no matter how long it takes. Keep God's vision clearly before your eyes. Find God's purpose for your life and focus intently upon it. God is never late. He will show up at the right time. Patience is a necessary virtue one has to possess when learning to rule as an eagle.

Finally, the fifth step in understanding how to rule as an eagle is for you to get up and do what you need to do and stop making excuses. In other words, I need to learn to use what is at my disposal. Returning to Moses (Exodus 3), he had everything he needed to carry out his vision, but he began to behave as a chicken instead of an eagle. Forty years earlier, Moses had run away from Egypt after killing an Egyptian, and when God announced it was time to go back, Moses complained he was not prepared to lead the Children of Israel from Egypt to the Promised Land as per God's directive. God finally asked him, "Moses, what do you have in your hands?" We usually make excuses like Moses and try to avoid learning how to fly or rule like an Eagle as God has destined. We give all the excuses we can find in the world. We state all the reasons why we are incapable of accomplishing our vision. I believe that sometimes the Lord sits and disappointingly says: "If only you knew what I have given to you. If only you knew how I have placed in you the ability to rule this earth. If only you knew how much I have invested in you. If only you knew that creation is awaiting your manifestation. If only you knew what it took to get you this far and how little of an effort is required to get you over." Some of us need to pray that the Lord would open our eyes for us to see. Elisha had to pray that prayer for his servant who was afraid when he saw the king's soldiers (II Kings 6:17).

Like Moses, there are six general types of excuses we make. The first excuse is the "Who Me" Excuse (Exodus 3:11-12). Moses expressed his doubt in his ability by asking God, "Who am I that I should go to Pharaoh?" Moses probably recalled his abysmal failure when, 40 years earlier, he attempted to settle a dispute between an Egyptian and an Israelite. Moses did not like the thought of failing again. The devil wants us to believe that we are failures and he will do everything to convince us of that lie. He wants us to believe that our past is not redeemable or forgivable. He wants us to believe that we are not good enough and do not have what it takes to get the job done. He wants us to believe that we do not have the education that is required or that we are not smart enough. He wants us to believe that we are second-class citizens because of our background and experience. These are lies from the pit of hell. Your past does not determine your future. It is God who knows and holds the future. In fact, your days ahead may be better than the ones that have already passed. God was saying to Moses, "If you doubt yourself, then lean on me. I will be there for you and I will help." That is what a parent eagle says to its eaglet. The parent eagle tells the child, "I will be there for you as you learn to fly. As you learn to rule the sky, I will be by your side; I am not leaving you helpless and defenseless."

It is comforting to know that God says the same thing to us today when we do not trust ourselves. He does not condemn us. He simply says, "Cast all of your cares upon me because I care for you" (I Peter 5:7).

The second excuse we often give to God when He sends us out to rule is the "Whose Authority" excuse –the same excuse Moses offered to the Lord (Exodus 3:13-15). He asked what He should say to the children of Israel were they to ask for the name of God. Moses wanted to know the authority under which he was going to operate. What is interesting is the fact that Moses already knew the answer but was finding a way not to go. All he needed to do was to remind himself of the One with whom he was speaking, and he would have immediately remembered the scope of His authority. This is exactly what we must do; we must not allow the devil to intimidate us or cause us to live like chickens (remain earthbound), but remember who our Father is and begin to fly upwards, towards the heavens. When we remember who our God is, then we will mount up with wings like an eagle and soar, conquering the sky. We must remember that our God controls everything, even life and death. He has authority over life and death. Jesus passed on this authority to His disciples. Days after His glorious resurrection He stated, "I have given you authority to trample on snakes and scorpions and to overcome all the power of the enemy; nothing will harm you."[53] When you have doubt about your ability, remember the Lord's ability. When you have doubt about your strength, remember the Lord's strength. When you have doubt about your knowledge, remember the Lord knows all things and absolutely nothing is hidden from Him. When you have doubt about under whose authority you are operating, remember that you are operating under the authority of the Lord of Host; He who has never lost a battle; He who knows the end from the beginning; He who holds the heart of a king in His hands; He who was, and is and is to come. That is what God said to Moses. Tell them, "I Am that I Am." God was literally saying, "I am He who was, and is and always shall be!" or "I will continue to be what I have always been."

---

[53]   Luke 10:19

The third excuse we often give is the "What if" excuse (4:1-9). Moses started to question the Lord by asking a hypothetical question, "What if they don't believe me or don't want to listen to me?" That is a flimsy excuse. The reverse is also true, "What if they do believe and listen?" You need to realize that "what ifs" are dream killers, victory assassins, zeal slayers, faith destroyers, success predators, and reality stealers. Moses became so troubled by what may possibly happen that he was not able to focus on the actual presence of God or the signs the Lord had shown to him. For instance, God commanded Moses to throw down his staff (a simple enough command), but surprisingly, it turned into a serpent (Exodus 4:2-3). Next, the Lord commanded Moses to pick the serpent up by its tail (Exodus 4:4). What! Being told to pick up a serpent by its tail is a much more difficult command—something most people do not want to do! In fact, when the staff turned into a serpent, Moses ran for his life. He probably saw that the serpent was a dangerous one. Yet, when God told him to pick it up by its tail, Moses obeyed. In case that sign was not enough, the Lord provided another sign, causing Moses' hand to become leprous then whole again (Exodus 4: 6-7). Despite these miracles, Moses still asked his "What if" question.

The fourth excuse that we give the Lord is "I speak funny, I have an accent, or I am not a good communicator." Moses tried this same excuse on God: "O Lord, I have never been eloquent, neither in the past nor since you have spoken to your servant; but I am slow of speech and tongue" (Exodus 4:10). This may look or sound like a valid excuse to us except it contradicts Stephen's report; Moses, raised as a son of royalty for the first forty years in Egypt, was a man "educated in all the wisdom of the Egyptians and was powerful in speech and action" (Acts 7:22). The Lord responded to Moses' complaint by reminding him that He, God, made man's mouth and is the one who makes people mute, deaf, blind or cripple. Hence, He instructed Moses to get up and go. He was simply telling Moses, it is time to get out of your eagle's nest and begin to fly. It is time to lead and rule. It is time to set wrong right. It is time to bring my people out of captivity. It is time to see and know that I am God. It is time for Me to display My power among other "gods."

You and I need to understand that the Lord has called us to rule, and our perceived inadequacies are not sufficient reasons for which the Lord cannot use us. The Lord knows all about our "deficiencies," and He has already factored those into His perfect plans for our life. God made us the way we are and if He has called us to do a particular job, He will provide all that is necessary for us to be successful in accomplishing His assigned task.

That was God's verdict to Moses; if I give you a task, I will empower you to accomplish it. Unfortunately, it appeared as if Moses was not convinced or maybe he had real difficulty getting rid of the chicken mentality. Having exhausted all known excuses, Moses revealed his attitude of entrenched, outright rejection of God's plan. He as much as stated, "Lord, I refuse to leave this eagle nest, period." You can pull out all the nesting material from under me, show me all the flying tricks, describe how You will use me to work miracles and all that stuff, but I am not going anywhere. Finally, Moses pleaded with God, "Send someone else" (Exodus 4:13). "Then the Lord's anger burned against Moses" (Exodus 4:14). Why was God so angry? Moses was selfish in considering that his response to God was only about him. Far from it! When we say "no" to God, we discourage God's people who are counting on our obedience. Additionally, making excuses hinders you from attaining God's best and forces a few people to carry the weight of the many. You need to realize that no one can fly for you. No one can perform the task that the Lord has ordained for you better than you can. No one can fulfill God's plan and purpose for your life better than you can. No one can fly in your place. Each eaglet has to learn to fly and take its rightful place in the sky. Even when God agreed to a compromise with Moses and brought his brother Aaron into the picture, we quickly see that it was less than God's best. In the first place, when they arrived in Egypt, Moses did all the talking and not a word was heard from Aaron. In Exodus 32, it was Aaron who led the people of God into idol worship when Moses went up on Mount Sinai for forty days to receive the Ten Commandments from the Lord. It is Aaron and Miriam who, seeking equality with Moses, criticized him and drew down the wrath of God upon themselves (Numbers 12:1-3). We can therefore conclude that God's perfect will is always better than His permissive will!

In conclusion, remember that in order to learn how to fly as an eaglet, you must correctly heed the imprinting process, be willing to learn and submit to teaching, take the initiative to find a suitable, wise mentor, and fully cooperate with God to be all He created you to be for His glory and the good of His people. In addition, it is extremely important for you to know yourself by understanding your strengths, weaknesses and areas of potential growth and development and finally, stop making excuses. God is angered and disappointed by our excuses and Satan rejoices over them. You must stop procrastinating, end your habit of making excuses for disobedience to God, and instead do as He has instructed. When you step out in faith, the Lord will honor you. The Lord is calling you to step out of the nest. Can you not hear Him calling? It is time to take your place in God's kingdom and stop living as a second-class citizen!

CONCLUSION

UNDERSTANDING THE MOLTING STAGE

"Praise the Lord, my soul, and forget not all his benefits—
who forgives all your sins and heals all your diseases,
who redeems your life from the pit and crowns you with
love and compassion, who satisfies your desires with good
things so that your youth is renewed like the eagle's"
(Psalms 103:2-5).

There can come a time in the life of a believer when a period of discouragement or questioning faith itself can lead to a loss of interest in the things of God. I equate these symptoms to those of going through a spiritual heart attack (which will be the next book that I plan to write by the grace of God). These "dark valley experiences" could be a direct result of not receiving the answer to a request, becoming overwhelmed by a spiritual attack of the enemy, or the aftermath of suffering a crisis in life (job loss, financial crisis, or the death of a loved one). These "dark valley experiences" can catch us unaware because they sometimes occur after a major spiritual victory against the enemy. Immediately after the celebration, the believer sinks into a valley. The Children of Israel had that experience. Days after God's people victoriously passed through the Red Sea on dry land, they found themselves dying of thirst from not locating a water source for three days. Finally, water was discovered at Marah, but it was far too bitter to drink (Exodus 15:22-24). They started to grumble against Moses. This is truly a "valley experience" immediately following the jubilant time of praise and worship when the entire assembly, led by Miriam, danced in the presence of the Lord for the miraculous works He had done. In 1 Kings 19:1-5, we also read about Elijah's flight to Horeb after being threatened by Jezebel. Elijah had a "mountain top experience" when he called down fire from heaven and four hundred and fifty prophets of Baal were subsequently killed. But the heights of victory reversed to the lows of depression when Elijah received a message from Jezebel, the wife of King Ahab, saying, "May the gods deal with me, be it ever so severely, if by this time tomorrow I do not make your life like that of one of them" (1 Kings 19:2). In fear, Elijah ran for his life. Elijah had just experienced the mighty power of God, but turned and ran from a woman who really could not do anything to him because of God's call, anointing and protections upon his life.

When one experiences a spiritual heart attack, he is unable to reason properly. Dejected, Elijah said to God, "Lord, I have had enough. Take my life; I am no better than my ancestors." Elijah was discouraged, tired, frustrated, hungry, exhausted, lonely, afraid, and in the midst of a spiritual heart attack. He no longer had an interest in serving as God's spokesperson. He did not have any interest in God using him to perform miracles. He did not want to have anything to do with the people of God. He no longer had any interest in human relationship and it appears as if he did not want anyone around him either; Elijah left his servant at Beersheba in Judah and ventured another day's journey into the desert all by himself. Elijah, God's choice eaglet, no longer delighted in flying or soaring the sky. He collapsed and buried his head between his knees; he no longer wanted to live. The Apostle Paul faced similar opposition, but responded with more fortitude, "We are hard pressed on every side, but not crushed; perplexed, but not in despair; persecuted, but not abandoned; struck down, but not destroyed" (2 Corinthians 4:8). Paul freely admits that living as a Christian may involve pressing, bamboozling, persecuting, and a being struck down. Some Christians face horrible moments of trial and uncertainty.

Eagles have a period in their lifecycle that roughly corresponds to what I have just described, known as the Molting Stage. Molting is a stage of discouragement, followed by renewal and restoration.

The molting stage is characterized by:

1) The feathers of the eagle fall off: The feathers of an eagle become dull over time and it gradually loses its ability for a brief period to fly high into the sky.
2) Build-up of Calcium in its beak: Calcium begins to build up in the eagle's beak resulting in its inability to hold up its heads, or look into the sky.
3) The talons lose their strength: The eagle's talons lose their strength and power during the molting stage, making it difficult to hunt. The majestic creature that lives on fresh meat now has to survive on scraps, but just for a little while.

As a result, the eagle becomes depressed during the molting stage and has to wait for its body to rejuvenate.

During the molting state, an eagle's survival depends on four factors:

A) The environment the eagle chooses for its molting stage (a place that is safe and where it can receive direct sun light).
B) The involvement and encouragement the eagle receives from its community.

C) The attitude the eagle exhibits towards recovery.

D) The eagle's ability to be patient and allow its body to function as God has created it.

When God's eaglets are pressured, pressed, persecuted, and pursued, we could say they are going through their molting stage or the storm of life. Unfortunately, some of us allow the storm to kill us, because God does not always calm the storm; yet, sometimes He seeks to calm His child in the midst of the storm.

Here are some very important facts about storms in life. The first is that storms will come, whether we like them or not. Secondly, some storms are unavoidable; you cannot run, walk away or hide from them. Therefore, develop in yourself a positive, hopeful attitude towards trials; willing to face life "head on" and not hiding out as an "avoider" or "quitter" when things get tough. Thirdly, some storms arrive un-expectantly, seeming to appear out of nowhere, finding us unprepared. Fourthly, some storms are severe, shaking us to our core, challenging our faith, testing our resolve, and seeking to define our character. Fifthly, the storms of life arrive during various "seasons" of life. Some are very dangerous while others are not that bad. What is most important is not the intensity of the storm but your reaction to it. You can decide to react in fear or in faith. It is your reaction that will determine the affect of the storm on your life.

During my past twenty-four years of serving the Lord, I have noticed that at any given moment I am either recovering from a storm, in the midst of a storm, or just entering a storm. In other words, storms are a part of life. Additionally, I have concluded that some storms are natural whereas others are supernatural. Some are a direct result of the atmospheric conditions, whereas others have a direct link to the supernatural world.

We should remember that when a physical storm arrives, it affects everyone within that locality irrespective of education, color, belief, or financial standing. The storm has no ability to single out an individual for better or worse treatment.

Jesus told His disciples a parable about two men, one wise and one foolish, who built houses with two different types of foundations (Luke 6:47-49). What distinguished the two men was not their physical appearance, education, or the fact that they decided to build two separate houses; it was their decision regarding the foundations of their houses—one chose to build on the sand and the other chose to build on the rock. Being wise or being a fool, Jesus seems to imply, depends on the foundational decisions we make in life. In addition, Jesus noted that the storm came. For Him, it was not a question of whether it will come, how it will come, when it will come, or where it will strike. The focus of His parable was on the readiness of both men for the arrival of the storm. Storms come to everybody, but sometimes they approach us by surprise. A storm can be more than an "an atmospheric disturbance manifested in strong winds accompanied by rain, snow, or other precipitation and often by thunder and lightning."[54] It could simply be a metaphor referring to a complex or insurmountable challenge in one's marriage, job, body, family, etc. When you encounter this type of storm, you may become depressed and enter your molting stage. It may seem that your dreams and aspirations are destroyed and all hope in the future is lost; years of labors and investments are shattered overnight, sometimes while you slept. The Bible says that the enemy comes and sows seeds while we sleep (Matthew 13:25). But, I want to tell you that some storms can be prevented if we are not "sleeping." Jesus admonished His disciples to not sleep but to watch and pray (Mark 14:32-42). Your marriage does not have to end in divorce. That financial problem does not have to lead you to your grave. You do not have to

---

[54] The American Heritage® Dictionary of the English Language, Fourth Edition copyright ©2000 by Houghton Mifflin Company. Updated in 2009. Published by Houghton Mifflin Company.

let stress and worry lead to a heart attack or stroke. Some storms are preventable and for others we can minimize their effects. Though an eagle experiences the distressing symptoms of molting, this stage does not need to lead to the eagle's death.

The Israelite judge, Samson, (Judges 16), experienced a series of storms in his life because of his own foolish choices. Samson's life did not have to end the way it did. His eyes did not have to be plucked out of his head. He did not have to play the role of a fool in a Philistine's prison and he certainly did not have to suffer the kind of humiliation he suffered at the hands of his enemies after being used mightily by the Lord to bring judgment to Israel's enemies. His problem was his environment, his affiliates, his attitude, and his lack of acceptance of God's word. His "storm" was a product of his fleshly desires and decisions. Samson allowed pride, lust, and rage to determine his reaction to his "storm" instead of his faith. His life is a testimony of how *not* to "weather a storm." As God's eaglets, some of the storms we encounter are preventable, but we need to do our part by keeping our eyes on Christ; unfortunately, sometimes we do not.

I believe that the molting stage is not really about those storms that are preventable because there is actually nothing the eagle can do to prevent that stage. I am of the conviction that the molting process has to do with those storms that are unforeseeable, unpredictable, and unavoidable. It has to do with those storms that are supernatural in design and origin. It is about those storms that are designed by the enemy to destroy your faith and knock you out of the race. They are those "fiery furnace storms" intended to put you on public display, show that your faith is worthless, castigate your testimony, and defame the name of the God you serve. That is exactly what Nebuchadnezzar tried to do to the three Hebrew boys: Shadrach, Meshach, and Abednego (Daniel 3:19-30). He ordered that the furnace be heated seven times hotter than usual. The fire was so hot that it killed the soldiers who threw the boys into it. How hot is your fire? It does not have to consume you. The same God that the Hebrew boys served is still available in His power, majesty and glory.

Do not be like the man who built his house upon the sand. Sand, which is a collection of loose grains of worn or disintegrated rock, represents something that is on the surface, moving, shifting, changing, and unstable. When the wind came, the foolish man's house fell because its foundation was shifting, changing and unstable. The house was destroyed because it had a foundation problem. On the contrary, Jesus said that the wise man dug down deep and laid his foundation on the rock. The wise man understood that if his house were to survive a storm, it had to have the right foundation. Hence, he paid attention to and fortified that which the foolish man could not see—the foundation.

While an eagle is trudging through the molting stage, it finds a place, safe and isolated, lies on a rock and relies on the sun to shine directly upon it. It spends time in the sun, recuperating. Jesus spent thirty years of His life laying the foundation for a mere three and a half years of ministry. From the scriptures, we have information only about His birth and a brief account when He was twelve years old. For thirty years He diligently built a sturdy, yet hidden foundation. He built the right foundation as He patiently prepared for the Father's perfect timing. When His mother brought to his attention the lack of wine at the wedding in Cana of Galilee, He replied, "My time has not yet come" (John 2:4). Like the wise man in the parable, Jesus invested His time and effort in building a good foundation even though He was the Word that became flesh and dwelled among men.

Digging a deep foundation requires money, time, energy, and technical skills. The wise man was willing to dig deep. When one is digging deep, he does not have the time to complain, gossip, murmur, jump, shout, dance, watch television or play video games. An individual who is digging deep to lay the right foundation digs past all the debris that obscure the rock. Some of the debris that we must dig through are feelings, emotions, popular opinions, religious pedigrees, head knowledge, and cultural norms that violate the Word of God. When an eagle is about to go through the molting stage, it knows where to go and who to tell. It does not tell everyone because it realizes that if it does, sooner or later it will become a prey for other predators. Most importantly, it does not go to a place filled with sand. Rather, the eagle seeks the proper foundation, a rock. When it finds the rock, it rests on the rock.

Edward Mote said, "One morning it came into my mind as I went to labor, to write a hymn on the 'gracious Experience of a Christian.' As I went up Holborn, I had the chorus."[55] That chorus in Mote's head was, "On Christ the solid rock I stand. All other ground is sinking sand." Jesus is that rock that we need to withstand the storm and revive us when we are in our molting stage. In II Samuel 22:2, we read, " . . . The Lord is my rock and my fortress and my deliverer." The psalmist David wrote, "He only is my rock and my salvation: He is my defense; I shall not be moved" (Psalms 63:6). David also testified, "He lifted me out of the slimy pit, out of the mud and mire; He set my feet on a rock and gave me a firm place to stand" (Psalms 40:2). What an assurance!

---

[55] http://www.cyberhymnal.org/htm/m/y/myhopeis.htm. Retrieved June 8, 2012.

God did the lifting after He saw our condition. He established the rock upon which we need to stand. It is no wonder the psalmist boldly declared, "God is our refuge and strength, an ever-present help in trouble. Therefore we will not fear, though the earth give way, and the mountains fall into the heart of the sea, though its waters roar and foam and the mountains quake with their surging" (Psalms 46:1-3). You must discover Jesus who is THE ROCK and rest on or in Him. When you are standing firmly on the rock, Christ, it does not matter whether you are in a storm that was avoidable or one that is a direct result of your disobedience to God; either way, you are standing on the ROCK. That ROCK is stronger than the storm. It is even higher than the mountain you need to climb and deeper than the valley you need to cross. The rock can easily withstand the fire that is consuming you, and provide a defense against the flood in which you are drowning. It is stronger than the enemies that are pursuing you and yet peaceful as a dove. King David expressed this revelation so eloquently, "When my heart is overwhelmed, lead me to the Rock that is higher than I."[56] That ROCK has the ability to produce water to quench your thirst as it did for over one million Israelites (Exodus 17:6-7). It has the ability to produce fire to consume as it did to Gideon's offering (Judges 6:21). In it, one can find rivers of oil (Job 29:6) and satisfying honey (Psalms

[56] Psalms 61:2

81:16). Paul confirms the identity of that ROCK which followed the children of Israel through the wilderness as Jesus Christ (I Corinthians 10:4). He is that ROCK that never rolls, moves, shifts, changes, or breaks. Jesus, the ROCK, is like a close friend that never abandons you and a captain that never sinks his ship.

The eagle's molting stage cannot be avoided but when it enters that stage, it can rely on the rock, the sun and the help other eagles offer. The eagle comes out of that "pit" thanks to the support it receives. You can make it as well because of the ROCK, the Son, and the body of Christ. Christ is the foundation upon which you need to build your house. When the storms of life come, and they will, your house will remain standing.

Do you want to fly as an eagle? Do you want to experience God's best? Do you want to rule and take your rightful place in the earth as God has destined before the foundation of the world? Do you want to be the kind of ambassador God has called you to be? Why not follow God's advice and learn from the animals? Through these animals, God has provided us the blueprints we need to rule this earth and live out His plans and purposes for our lives. Take the time to wait on the Lord and study some of the animals mentioned in the Bible (eagles, ants, donkey, calf, chicken, sheep, horse, lamb, and lion) that God has supplied for our instruction. I can guarantee you that you will be surprised by what the Lord will reveal to you. Wait upon the Lord and then mount up with wings like eagles. By so doing, you will run and not be weary and you will walk and not faint.

BIBLIOGRAPHY

Backstein, Karen. *The Blind Men and the Elephant*. New York: Scholastic, 1992.

Clinton, Robert J. *Mentoring: Developing Leaders Through Empowering Relationships.* Lecture at Calvin Seminary. Grand Rapids, Michigan, Altadena, CA: Barnabas Publisher, September 1998.

Gerrard, Jon M., and Bortolotti, Gary R. *The Bald Eagle: Haunts and Habits of a Wilderness Monarch*. Washington, DC: Smithsonian Books; 1st Edition, April 1988.

Gibbons, Gail. *Soaring With the Wind: The Bald Eagle*. New York, NY: HarperCollins, 1998.

Guidry, Jeff. *An Eagle Named Freedom: My True Story of a Remarkable Friendship*. New York, NY: William Morrow Paperbacks; Reprint edition. August 2011.

Howard, Josef A. *Turning Your Mess Into A Message*. Bloomington, Indiana: AuthorHouse, 2011.

Hunter, Charles and Frances. *Don't Limit God:* The Story of Gene Lilly. Houston, Texas: Hunter Ministries Publishing Company, 1976.

Hutchinson, Alan E. *Just Eagles: A Wildlife Watcher's Guide.* Minocqua, Wisconsin: Willow Creek Press, April 2000.

Jakes, T.D. *Maximize The Moment: God's Action Plan for Your Life.* New York, New York: Berkley Publishing Group, 1999.

Maxwell, John C. *Mentoring 101.* Nashville, Tennessee: Thomas Nelson; 1 edition. September 2008.

Mallison, John. *Mentoring to Develop Disciples and Leaders.* NSW, Australia: Scripture Union, 1998.

Smalley, Gary and Trent, John. *Love is a Decision: Thirteen Proven Principles to Energize Your Marriage and Family.* New York, New York: First Pocket Book Printing, January 1993.

Swanson, Diane. *Eagles: Welcome to the World Series.* North Vancouver, BC: Whitecap Books Ltd., January 1, 2010.

Swindoll, Charles R. *Start. Where You Are: Catch a Fresh Vision For Your Life.* Nashville, Tennesee: Word Publishing, 1999.

Tekiela, Stan. *Majestic Eagles: Compelling Facts and Images of the Bald Eagle*. Cambridge, Minnesota: Adventure Publications, March 2007.

Helpful websites:

Bald Eagles. Vision: An In-depth Look at Eagle Eyes. Http://www.learner.org/jnorth/tm/eagle/VisionA.html#Eyes. Retrieved May 19, 2011.

Eagles.
http://hubpages.com/hub/eagle-bird. Retrieved, May 10, 2011

Jeevanjal Ministries. Eagle Christian. http://www.jeevanjal.org/jeevanjal/eagle-christian.html. Retrieved February 4, 2012.

Ruth Commentary 1:14-18.
http://www.preceptaustin.org/ruth 114-22.htm. Retrieved January 16, 2012.

The Molting Process.
http://www.hopeinhull.com/Eagle%20Series.htm. Retrieved, February 3, 2012.

ABOUT THE AUTHOR

Dr. Josef A. Howard is an Ordained Minister of Bethel World Outreach Ministries International who currently serves as Resident Pastor of Bethel World Outreach Church, Robbinsdale, Minnesota. He heads the credential committee of Bethel World Outreach Ministries International (BWOMI). His primary responsibility is to ensure that ministers of BWOMI receive the necessary training and preparation required to serve God's people and, as such, supervises the process for licensing and ordination. Dr. Howard is also the former Executive Director of the Liberian Ministers Association, a religious, non-profit organization that serves Liberian pastors in Minnesota. He has been privileged to work for the last eight years as a chaplain at Regions Hospital in Saint Paul, Minnesota.

Rev. Josef A. Howard earned a Doctor of Philosophy (PhD) in Missiology with emphasis in Leadership Development from Concordia Theological Seminary in Fort Wayne, Indiana, a Master of Divinity in Pastoral Care from Bethel Theological Seminary in Arden Hills, Minnesota, and an advanced certificate in Biblical Studies and Preaching from the Monrovia Bible Training Center in Liberia, an affiliate of Living Word Missions, Massachusetts. He also holds a diploma in Cross Culture Ministry from Bethany College of Missions in Bloomington, Minnesota.

Additionally, Dr. Howard studied Business Administration and Economics at the University of Liberia, West Africa, and holds a Bachelor of Arts degree in French Studies from Universite Nationale de Cote d'Ivoire.

The author feels called by God as a West African missionary to the United States to help churches understand the richness found in multiculturalism and to explain how churches can overcome the challenges found therein. It is in this regard that he wrote his PhD dissertation on: "Challenges a non-Westerner faces in establishing a multicultural church in the United States."

A teacher, preacher, musician, author, conference speaker, chaplain, and trainer on church leadership, church ushering, multiculturalism, church growth, spiritual care-giving and spiritual warfare, Dr. Howard loves the Lord and has dedicated his life to help in the establishment of God's plan and will in the lives of His people and His church. He is of the opinion that nothing is impossible with God. If God has said it, He will surely bring it to pass. It is this message that forms the core of his ministry.

Dr. Howard is happily married to his lovely and charming wife, Lees Howard, and they have been blessed with four biological children (Nancy, Cecil, Caleb, and Marylyn) and several adopted and spiritual children.

CPSIA information can be obtained
at www.ICGtesting.com
Printed in the USA
FFHW021634161218
49891605-54491FF

9 781481 762854